DELPHINIUMS

DELPHINIUMS

THE COMPLETE GUIDE

Colin Edwards
Vice-President of the Delphinium Society

The Crowood Press

First published in 1989 by
The Crowood Press Ltd
Ramsbury, Marlborough
Wiltshire SN8 2HR

Paperback edition 1995

British Library Cataloguing in Publication Data
A catalogue record for this book is available from the British Library.

ISBN 1 85223 891 7

Acknowledgements

Photographs by Nigel Moody
Line illustrations by Sharon Perks

Typeset by Footnote Graphics, Warminster, Wiltshire
Printed in Great Britain by Redwood Books, Trowbridge, Wiltshire

Contents

Acknowledgements

Without my library of the Delphinium Society's year books, which cover sixty years, much of these contents could not have been written. My grateful thanks are due to all the contributors, both past and present.

To Nigel Moody, with whom I have shared for many years a mutual love of the delphinium. I am indebted for his agreement to prepare a series of photographs specially for this book.

To all my friends in the Delphinium Society, some of whom I have had for over thirty-five years, I am grateful for their help.

Most of all, I extend my heartfelt gratitude to my wife, not only for her help and typing the manuscript, but also for tolerating my addiction to the delphinium.

Foreword

I have known Colin Edwards since 1959 when he joined the General Committee of the Delphinium Society. His uncle, the late Mr H R Lucas, was also a keen delphinium enthusiast, Honorary Secretary of the Society and the editor of the Society's *Year Book*, which has been quite outstanding for many years and is still of a very high quality. In 1963 Colin became honorary Show Secretary until 1966, remaining a member of the General Committee from 1967 to 1976, and in 1977 he became Treasurer. He also joined the Joint Delphinium Committee in 1977, and became involved in scrutinising the new cultivars that are submitted either for an Award of Merit for Exhibition or for selection for trial at the Royal Horticultural Society's gardens at Wisley.

In 1978, besides the post of Treasurer, he took on the job of Membership Secretary with his wife and became editor of the Year Book for 1978 and 1979. In 1981, Colin became the Secretary of the Society, a post which he held until 1986, whilst his wife Joan carried on as Membership Secretary until 1983 when she handed over to Mrs Shirley Bassett.

Besides all the excellent work which he has carried out on behalf of the Society, Colin also decided to propagate a number of named cultivars of the delphinium – during his period in office with the Society, the specialist firms in this beautiful flower had reduced in number from four or five to just one. He also turned his hand to raising new varieties, and persuaded Ian Butterfield, of Butterfields Nursery in Buckinghamshire (also a specialist grower of pleiones and dahlias), to take over his collection of named cultivars, and helped him with the propagating until he was established.

When I became President of the Society in 1978, I urged it to form a Breeders Committee to encourage all members with named cultivars to propagate some and distribute their plants in certain areas of the country. I am glad to say that this has worked out well and, with three specialist firms and such keen amateurs as Colin Edwards, Dr Clive Rowe and Dr and Mrs Bassett, the future of the Delphinium Society and flower itself will continue to flourish.

At the Annual General Meeting of the Society in November 1987, Colin Edwards was awarded the position of Vice-President in recognition of his fine efforts on behalf of the Society for a great many years. I trust he will enjoy this deserved award for many years to come.

Stuart Ogg VMH
President of the Delphinium Society

Introduction

'What fantastic lupins!' This was the understandable gross error I made some forty years ago when I saw for the first time high-quality delphiniums growing in the garden of an uncle. His reply is best left unsaid, but you can imagine its tone, since he was at that time Secretary of the Delphinium Society. Years later, whilst assisting on a stand of delphiniums at the Chelsea Flower Show, I had sympathy for those members of the public (and there were quite a number), who knowledgeably said to friends that our flowers were blue hollyhocks or even a 'new race of giant foxgloves'. Mistakes in recognising the genus like these do not really surprise me, for a properly-grown named delphinium, which has been registered with and received an award from the Royal Horticultural Society, is so vastly superior to most, if not all, those plants obtainable from non-specialist sources that to the uninitiated it really does seem to be a different flower.

Many gardeners who choose hardy perennial flowers do so not only to enjoy a colourful display, but also because they want a long-lived plant and one which does not have to be constantly lifted and divided. In addition, many gardeners, especially younger ones it seems, are looking for quick results, and their ideal is a plant which will grow happily in any type of soil and thrive relatively free of pests and diseases. The delphinium fulfils all these attributes and with a proper choice of cultivars the season of this flower can be surprisingly long.

The delphinium is often referred to in books on general gardening as the 'Queen of the Border' – a fitting description of this stately genus. The flowers range in colour from blue and white, through the mauves, to very dark purple. Dusky pinks are now also common, and there are even those which almost give an appearance of yellow. It may not be many years before other warmer colours, such as red and orange, become available.

Many first-time gardeners, after maintaining a garden as a pleasant place in which to relax and an area where the children can 'let off steam', soon find the urge to specialise in

9

a particular flower which takes their fancy. To these gardeners the flower of their choice so often becomes an absorbing hobby and one which can become very fulfilling and it is not hard to see why so many choose the delphinium. I know of no other plant which responds so well to a little extra care and attention, or which can be so easily propagated. Perhaps most importantly of all, the delphinium can provide, at very modest expense, some truly wonderful plants from seed when the correct selection is made.

This specialisation soon leads to an enthusiasm for hybridisation – it is an easy matter to cross one delphinium with another, and this leads to another exciting branch of the pastime. The keen gardener may even become attracted to the show bench, although it must be said that there are many enthusiasts who prefer to leave their delphiniums in the garden, where they can enjoy them for a longer period.

The delphinium will bloom whether it is cared for or not, but the enthusiast can transform the miserable specimens that you see growing in some gardens (which have probably been purchased from a non-specialist source) to ones of outstanding magnificence with a minimum of effort and expense. I believe the following chapters will demonstrate this fact.

1

The History and Development

It is amusing to consider that the first documented evidence of the delphinium does not record it as the strikingly lovely flower we know today, but as a medicine used as a cure for a scorpion bite. About two thousand years ago, Pedanios Dioscorides, a Greek serving under Emperor Nero, compiled his famous *Materia Medica*, a medical register of efficacious herbs, in which he noted that the seeds of the species *D. staphisagria* were effective as an antidote against the venom of the scorpion. It has always been an ambition of mine to lay eyes on the entry – I understand that the original manuscript may be seen to this day in the Vienna State Library.

Another species, *D. peregrinum*, was also recorded at the same time and, because the bud of the individual flower resembled a dolphin, the modern name 'delphinium' evolved from the Greek for 'a little dolphin'.

There are many hundreds of different species of the delphinium scattered widely throughout the world, and almost invariably their habitat is in mountainous areas. There is, however, only one recorded species indigenous to the British Isles and that is the wild larkspur, known botanically today as *D. ajacis*. The familiar name 'larkspur' was given because it was thought that the opened flower resembled the spur of the lark.

(It must be mentioned that it is a daunting task to be accurate when dealing with the history and the recording of the species of a particular flower, for it is clear from my researches that over-zealous botanists, particularly in the early Victorian period, were guilty of naming species delphiniums that had been already 'discovered' by others. This gave rise to many synonyms.)

The delphinium that is commonly cultivated throughout the world today is known as an 'elatum delphinium', although this name is both misleading and inaccurate. To

11

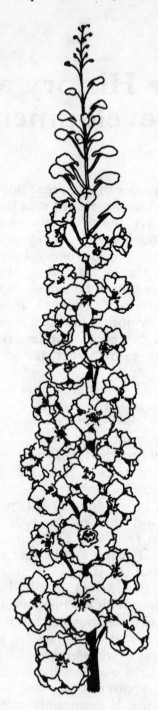

A delphinium spike with well-shaped florets.

unravel the mystery of how such a false name should have arisen we have to refer to the eighteenth century, when the French horticulturalist, Vilmorin Andrieux, offered to the general public seed of the species *D. elatum*, which is pale blue and is still widely distributed in Europe and Asia.

It was soon grown alongside two other species – the violet *D. formosum* and the mid-blue *D. grandiflorum*. As a result hybrids occurred, probably without the assistance of artificial cross-pollination, and the offspring which resulted from the juxtaposition of these three species led to an improved race of plants. It was at this point that the new hybrids were referred to as 'elatums', almost certainly because the hybridised seed was collected from the prolific seed bearer *D. elatum*. The term 'elatum' has remained in common usage until this day.

THE PROFESSIONALS AND HYBRIDISATION

Lemoine and Kelway

It was not until the middle of the nineteenth century that the first serious attempts were made to improve the delphinium by hybridisation. The work of the French nurseryman, Victor Lemoine, was outstanding – his nursery produced hundreds of hybrids of advanced stature as well as colour from around 1850 until the turn of the century. His hybrids caused such a sensation that they were soon in great demand outside France, and one shrewd English nurseryman, James Kelway, quickly imported to Britain the best of Lemoine's plants. Notable among the imports was a plant regarded as a milestone in the development of the flower. This fine delphinium, named 'Statuaire Rudé', was semi-double with 3in (7.5cm) florets and of a beautiful heliotrope colour. This delphinium, together with a plum-coloured hybrid raised by Kelway and named 'King of Delphiniums', formed the basis of much nineteenth-century hybridisation and it is safe to hazard a guess that these two early hybrids are the ancestors of many of our modern cultivars.

Blackmore and Langdon

It often happens in horticulture that luck or chance can play a considerable part in success. It was chance that led to the raising of a sensational delphinium around 1895 by a nurseryman from Bath, who was given a tray of seedlings by one Charles Langdon. The result of one seedling was an outstanding flower, and it was immediately named 'Revd E Lascelles'. You can judge the merits of this delphinium, which was royal blue with a contrasting white eye, from the fact that it gained an Award of Merit from the Royal Horticultural Society in 1907, and was continually offered for sale until around 1960. Of greater significance was the fact that the donor, Charles Langdon, was the gardener to the Revd Lascelles. He became so interested in the delphinium that, together with Mr JB Blackmore, he formed in 1901 what was to become the most famous specialist delphinium nursery in the world – Blackmore & Langdon.

It is hard to exaggerate the tremendous influence that this nursery has had on the improvement and popularity of the delphinium. There can be few visitors to the Chelsea Flower Show each year who are not astonished by the magnificent display of modern cultivars on Blackmore & Langdon's stand, and a visit to their nursery near Bristol in June and July is rewarded by the sight of thousands of superbly-grown spikes, most of which are a result of their own breeding programme.

Blackmore & Langdon were the leaders in the field of introducing new cultivars, particularly during the two world wars when they made available for sale no less than about 150 new introductions. However, there were others who tried to satisfy for a period of almost a decade the insatiable demand for more and better plants from the wealthy owners of large gardens and estates. As a result of this demand many hundreds of inferior hybrids were foisted on the public and only a few plant breeders produced delphiniums comparable to those from the Blackmore & Langdon nursery.

However, there were exceptions. For example, Blackmore & Langdon were so impressed with the hybridisation carried out by Mr C Ferguson, an amateur living in Wadebridge, Surrey, that they acquired four plants from him, which had won awards from the Royal Horticultural Society during the period from 1912 to 1920, and added them to their own collection.

Frank Bishop

Around 1930, another amateur, Frank Bishop of Windsor, began a programme of delphinium breeding. He was so successful that he eventually joined Baker's nursery, shortly after the Second World War, giving up his career as a stonemason. His aim was to produce a race of delphiniums of a true blue character, and to this end he got his results.

Although Bishop did produce some truly wonderful blue shades, which were much sought after in their time, he also found during his breeding programme other seedlings of merit, mainly pastel shades. As a separate and independent line of breeding he continued to develop these other shades, and subsequently released through Baker's nursery a number of plants which were given the general description of the 'Commonwealth strain'.

It is sad to relate that however lovely and unique in colour the Bishop range of plants were, the constitution of many was doubtful. A large proportion were short-lived, failing to survive for long before degeneration took place and the stock became progressively weaker. I think it is true to say that most, if not all, have now disappeared from cultivation. Perhaps, unlike Blackmore & Langdon, Bishop concentrated on colour at the expense of longevity. Blackmore & Langdon, especially under the founder, were scrupulous in rejecting plants, however lovely, which were not truly perennial, and only retained those which were known to be of strong constitution. This aspect of their work is evidenced by the fact that many of their introductions that were raised decades ago are still available for sale and have shown little deterioration.

Other plant breeders were actively engaged during the same period in pursuit of separate lines in their breeding progammes, and although several plants of merit appeared on the market none survived long enough to challenge the work of Blackmore & Langdon seriously.

Frank Reinelt

Far away from the European scene there was some astonishing breeding being carried out in the USA. The Czechoslovakian Frank Reinelt, who emigrated to California in 1925, began a programme of line breeding which overshadowed the work of all the European breeders put together. Some idea of the enormous number of plants involved may be had from the fact that about 300 pounds of seed were required annually to satisfy the demand from American horticultural seedsmen. When you consider that about 10,000 seeds are needed to make up every ounce, you can readily appreciate the vast numbers of plants required for the annual seed harvest.

However, the aim of the Europeans and that of Frank Reinelt were very different. The climate of California is much more favourable than that of Great Britain, and its clemency led to a race of delphiniums which were to become known as 'Pacific giants' or 'Pacific strain'. These are still sold, both in plant form and as seeds, by the professional horticulturalists of Europe. In California the average temperature is such that delphiniums can be grown for most of the twelve months in the year. It was therefore possible for Reinelt to raise plants from seed several times a year, and these plants in turn would give several flushes of bloom annually.

So these plants were fine for the American seed market, but no serious attempt was made to supply plants produced by vegetative means, nor was there any real attempt to conduct trials for the perenniality of the strain. As a result, constant improvement was made both in size and colour, but the progeny tended to develop 'annual' characteristics. This factor was appreciated shortly after the Second World War when a small quantity of seed was given by Reinelt to some members of the Delphinium Society for trial. Those of us who grew the seed were immediately impressed with the form and some of the really lovely pastel shades which were produced, although it was noted that many of the plants failed to survive fracture during the British summer storms. The real disappointment came the year after sowing, for the mortality rate during the winter was horrendously high. The conclusion that can be drawn without fear of contradiction is that the Pacific strain is quite unsuitable for the climate in Britain if a truly perennial delphinium is what you want.

Unfortunately, attracted by the pastel shades in the Pacific strain, some breeders used the plants together with the existing British strain, with the unhappy result that some of the 'annual' characteristics of Reinelt's strain were contained in the offspring. Frank Bishop must have used Pacific blood in his breeding programme, and this would account for their lack of vigour over a period of time, and the fact that pastel shades, which were until that period very rare, were much in evidence, especially in his 'Commonwealth' plants. Others, too, must have used Pacific blood in their work, which account for various cultivars having a poor constitution, as well as other maladies such as a proneness to mildew.

However, it would be unfair to let the judgement on Reinelt's work pass, from a European point of view, without emphasising the great part which he played in the vast improvement in colour range. Without doubt, his greatest contribution to the delphinium outside the USA was his introduction of seed which yielded dusky-pink colours. He was able to produce this colour, which hitherto was non-existent, by using the species *D. cardinale* as a parent. This truly pure scarlet delphinium grows profusely in parts of western America, but contains sixteen chromosomes, whereas the 'elatum' contains thirty-two. Such a cross is not possible in the ordinary way, but Reinelt may well have used the drug colchicine, derived from the autumn crocus (*colchicum*), which has the facility of breaking down certain plant tissues and altering the number of chromosomes. In this case it is proven that the use of colchicine will double the number of chromosomes in *D. cardinale* from sixteen to thirty-two, making a cross viable. Thus a race of so-called 'pink' delphiniums appeared from the Reinelt stable – the deep shades were named 'Astolat', and the pale ones 'Elaine'. You can appreciate the sensation which these colours caused in Britain at the time and they were soon used by amateurs as well as Blackmore & Langdon as part of a separate breeding programme. Thanks to Reinelt's system of line breeding the grower can be certain that crossing a pink with a pink will yield almost one hundred per cent pink offspring and much hybridising was, and still, is carried out in improving not only the colour, but, more importantly, the vitality and constitution. Such has been the advancement in this colour range that there are a number of these named plants available in Britain, both in the deep dusky-pink range as well as in the paler colours, which can be relied upon to perform well in our climate and to behave as successful perennial plants.

ENTER THE AMATEUR

Although the amateur plant breeder always made contributions to the development of delphiniums, it was the professional horticulturalist who had the greatest influence in the past. However, while the social conditions were changing in Britain after the last war, so too were British gardens. The great estates and the huge gardens of the wealthy were diminishing rapidly as family finances dwindled, and as a result the demand for delphiniums lessened to such an extent that many nurseries which hitherto provided quantities of plants were forced to close. Only a few firms were able to continue as before, and they found that demand was falling alarmingly.

With increasing leisure time, and the need for shorter, compact plants which would be more suitable for the ever-decreasing size of the gardens that we have today, the amateur suddenly had a vested interest in concentrating on breeding delphiniums of a much smaller overall length. Gone was the need for the enormously tall plants of yester-year, suitable for the back of herbaceous borders and re-quiring constant attention by the paid gardener of a large household – such plants have no place in the smaller, more compact plots of today – and it is thanks mainly to the amateur that there are now available plants which are thoroughly suitable for the little garden.

The first of this new generation of delphinium enthusiasts was the late Ronald Parrett, who soon became famous as a plant breeder of some note. He was an accountant by profession and worked for most of his career with the *Daily Express*. It is ironical (again, luck can deal an ace), that his finest plant, which he named 'Daily Express', came from a packet of seed which was purchased from Baker's nurseries and which must have contained open-pollinated seed from the stud of Frank Bishop. 'Daily Express' is a clear Cam-bridge blue with a contrasting white eye. When it was first introduced it produced very long spikes, but it has over the years degenerated. This is hardly surprising for it was raised nearly forty years ago.

Although Ronald Parrett raised many fine plants for which he received the highest awards, he is best remembered as the editor of a new-style year book for the Delphinium Society. His first production was in 1954 and it was revol-utionary in presentation and format. It had instant appeal with over two hundred pages and many illustrations, and was cleverly designed to appeal to the everyday gardener rather than the select few of a wealthy disposition. So successful was his publication that the membership of the society soared in his first year of office by around four hundred per cent. The format of the year book has since remained very similar as successive editors have always agreed that it is hard to improve on it.

The 'Loch' Series

Whilst there were other amateurs who successfully raised new cultivars, receiving awards after trial at Wisley, none can compare with the late Colonel Tom Cowan. He began hybridisation in his modest-sized garden in Ealing, London, around 1959. His main quest was for true blue and later for turquoise. He was highly successful with both colours, but in addition other colours appeared which were of fine quality and of sufficient merit to receive awards.

Perhaps Tom Cowan's finest achievement was a range of mainly blue delphiniums known as the 'Loch' series. Being a Scot he chose the names of many of Scotland's famous lochs for his plants, and of these 'Loch Nevis' was quite outstanding. It received an award in 1967 and is a pure pale blue. As a show plant it dominated the London scene for many years, for it produced large, well-formed spikes with a minimum of cultivation. But as a garden plant it is supreme. Even now, after twenty years, it still has that splendid characteristic of holding all the petals of the bottom florets until the top ones are open and, instead of the petals dropping, they tend to wither on the spike. Moreover, it is perhaps the strongest of all delphiniums that I have known. It withstands the strongest of winds even when saturated with rain, and I have yet to know of a spike which has broken in the severest of gales.

Among the other splendid plants which he raised was 'Spindrift'. This plant instantly appealed to floral arrangers for in most soils it produces a true turquoise colour with a noticeable green tint – a colour much loved in floral art. Again, this plant has stood the test of time, and over twenty years have passed since its introduction. It is still capable of winning on the show bench and its vigour remains as strong as ever.

In the recent past the number of successful amateur hybridists has increased considerably and new seedlings are being given preliminary awards by the Royal Horticultural Society every year with recommendations for trial at Wisley. Many have received the highest awards after trial, and are in every way improvements on those plants of yesteryear. Such is the astonishing interest in the hybridisation of the delphinium among amateurs that their contribution to the trials at Wisley has completely eclipsed that of the professional nurseryman. Even Blackmore & Langdon, who were supreme for so many decades, have virtually ceased to hybridise, leaving the amateur alone in this field.

THE RED DELPHINIUM

Also of great importance in the history of the development of the delphinium is the work carried our by the Dutchman, Dr R A H Legro, who until recently conducted all his trials at the Wageningen University in the Netherlands. His hybridisation is quite unique and follows different paths from those already mentioned.

In 1953 Bob Legro first contemplated the challenge to produce elatum-type delphiniums in colours other than blue, mauve, purple and white. The wild plants which he used in his endeavour to produce the warmer colours were the Californian orange-red *D. nudicaule*, which is short and has a branching habit, and *D. cardinale*, also a native of California, but much taller and a vivid scarlet. The crossing of these two species by Bob Legro was relatively easy, for they both have sixteen chromosomes. In order to use the progeny in further crosses with elatum hybrids, which have thirty-two chromosomes, it was necessary to use the drug colchicine, which, used in minute doses, can bring about tetraploid plants whose cell nuclei possess double the number of chromosomes. This was successful – the treatment achieved the required doubling, and the cross led to the first recorded hybrid of an elatum-like delphinium, bearing pinkish-red, semi-double florets but with the desirable thirty-two chromosomes.

Apart from using tissue culture, which was not then available, there are no real short cuts in hybridisation, especially when breaking new ground, and results are slow. The process of raising a completely new line of plants can be complicated, and this has been true of Bob Legro's work. It has been a case of slow but sure progress over the last thirty years, with a gradual improvement year by year both in colour range and in size.

The work in the glasshouses at the Wageningen University

by Bob Legro and his staff was funded by the Dutch government, but, unhappily, a few years ago the financial backing was withdrawn, placing Bob in a dilemma, facing the fact that his life-time endeavour may have to come to an abrupt end. Fortunately, the Royal Horticultural Society came to the rescue and placed at Bob's disposal a purpose-built glasshouse in their gardens at Wisley so that his work could continue. It is to his credit, and it is an insight into his dedication, that he is prepared to commute between the Netherlands and Wisley in order to supervise the continual process of crossing and selection which is still very active.

Those of us who have been privileged to witness over the years the progress made can see the great improvement brought about so painstakingly, and to see hundreds of elatum-type delphiniums in the glasshouse at Wisley in exotic shades of true pink, orange and red, with combinations and variations of these colours, is a wondrous sight. All are fully double, but rarely with an eye, and range in height of actual flower spike from 18in to 3ft (45–90cm).

All the hybridisation has been carried out under glass, in order that the valuable pollen may be protected from the weather and in order to make the cross in an environment that is more easily controlled. It follows that these 'university hybrids', which is the name given to this race of plants, are all pot-grown, and there has not been any trial carried out on a large scale in field conditions. There are still many years of continual line breeding ahead before we can all benefit from seeing these brilliant colours in our gardens. Producing these lovely hybrids under glass is one matter, but to have reliable long-lived plants, subject to the vagaries of our outdoor environment, is only a likelihood in future years.

FUTURE DEVELOPMENTS

It is hard to forecast the likely development of the delphinium in the future. The impression is that there will be a steady improvement rather than any sensational breakthroughs in form or colour. The trend towards shorter plants is already taking place and will undoubtedly continue, leading, I feel sure, to a race of plants requiring no support. If he embarks on hybridisation, any gardener will discover that it is very easy to produce new hybrids and that the personal satisfaction which can be gained from a simple breeding programme can be very rewarding. There is an opening for any amateur gardener to produce hybrids which can compete with established raisers. To this end more gardeners should be encouraged to widen their horticultural activities so that they may experience the thrill of naming a flower, and receiving an award from the Royal Horticultural Society after a seedling of their raising has successfully been judged a worthy new plant. They, too, could join the ranks of the many amateurs who have contributed to the improvement and development of the delphinium, and perhaps even find a place in the future history of the genus as a raiser of distinction.

2
Hybridisation

The pedigree of the elatum delphinium is a complex one. As a result, seed will produce plants of a variable character, unlike those resulting from specie seed which will, by and large, produce plants similar to the parent, if not identical. It is this variation which offers to the amateur hybridiser the chance of raising plants from seed, some of which may prove to be of real value, showing desirable characteristics different from those already in commerce.

SEED FORMATION

Before describing the process of hybridisation it is necessary to explain how seed is formed in the elatum delphinium. The biological structure of the part of a delphinium floret which forms seed is, as with any other flower, very complicated, but we need only refer to those aspects which affect hybridisation.

The seed offered for sale by seedsmen in Britain is open-pollinated seed – that is to say, seed which has set naturally on a delphinium floret without any interference from man. In simple terms, a delphinium floret will produce seed by fertilising itself, even without the assistance of insects, wind or rain, and it is therefore 'self-fertile'. To prove the truth of this statement, and emphasise this important factor, it may be of interest to have a look at the results of some experiments I conducted a number of years ago.

Long before any floret was opened from the bud stage, I enclosed the whole spike of a delphinium in a fine-weave nylon stocking. This, in turn, was protected from wind and rain. The spike continued to develop in this enclosed environment, and in due course flowered, and each and every floret produced seed. Alongside, I selected another spike on the same plant from which I removed the pollen-producing part, known as the anther, in its embyro stage. The spike continued to develop and flower in the ordinary way, but this time not one seed was produced even though, unlike its

23

neighbour, it had no protection from insects or from the weather. This was not strictly a controlled experiment, nor indeed did it have the benefit of a large-scale trial, but it proved to me that neither the weather nor insects (including the bee), have much bearing on the pollination of a delphinium (if they have any at all).

This factor is of tremendous importance to the delphinium hybridist, for if we remove the anthers of a floret in its undeveloped stage it will not produce pollen, but we can take ripe pollen from another floret on a different plant and use it as a substitute. This simple process is hybridisation.

WHAT TO IMPROVE

Long before he starts this process of hybridisation the raiser should consider what he wants to try and achieve. As a guide, let us consider the improvements which are likely to be worthwhile and desirable. I am the first to admit that, when it comes to colour, the old saying 'beauty is in the eye of the beholder' is as true of the delphinium as of any other subject. To give credence to this notion I can but mention that many years ago the fashion in delphiniums was for florets made up of several combinations of colours, sometimes disparagingly referred to by those of different taste as 'football jerseys'. On the other hand, in the recent past, the vast majority of amateur hybridists have concentrated on producing florets of one pure colour, with no adulteration or blend of other colours. So I can only suggest that you try to achieve whatever colour takes your fancy.

There is, however, a general consensus of opinion on the other desirable characteristics which should be the goal of every hybridist, the most important of which is constitution. It is no earthly good producing a hybrid, however beautiful it may be, if it fractures in the slightest puff of wind, is not perennial, suffers from mildew, or has an ugly floret placement. You should always have in mind the importance of vigour, perenniality, freedom from mildew and a symmetrical placement of florets. Size of florets is also important, for anything under 2½in (6.25cm) in diameter would be considered rather small by today's standards. Many specialists now consider that any delphinium which sheds its bottom florets before the top-most ones are open has a serious fault, and, if shedding florets were a factor, a hybrid would have to have exceptionally improved characteristics before it was retained. Such cultivars as 'Loch Nevis' remain in pristine condition for a long period and rather than dropping, their florets tend to wither on the plant. This is important, for example, for floral arrangement.

RECESSIVE QUALITIES AND DOMINANT FEATURES

Let us suppose that you like a certain cultivar in every way, but it has a weak stem which tends to break in high winds. You notice that another cultivar always survives summer storms. If you cross the two together perhaps you might successfully breed a race of plants with all the desirable characteristics, but with the additional improvement of a stronger stem. But don't get carried away, for unfortunately it is at this point that you must consider two other factors in plant breeding – recessive qualities and dominant features.

Because of the complicated hybrid nature of the genus, you will discover that certain characteristics tend to manifest themselves each time a particular plant is used as part of a cross. This can be used to your advantage. For example, if the selected parent always produces a strong stem in every cross with a different delphinium, you could be reasonably sure that this dominant feature would be repeated and your chance of raising seedlings from the cross would result in the desirable offspring. On the other hand, it may be the case that the other plant has recessive qualities and, as a result, all the admired attributes may disappear from the offspring. It should be emphasised that all the flower's characteristics, including colour, can be both recessive as well as dominant.

There is only one way you can be certain of not making mistakes, and that is to keep a stud book, so that each time a cross is made characteristics can be noted at flowering time of recessive and dominant features.

BREEDING

Back Crossing

Sometimes recessive qualities can reappear with dominant features disappearing when open-pollinated seed from the original cross is sown, and the progeny is crossed with the original parent which had the features which were wanted. As a counsel of perfection this process can be repeated, leading to a third or even fourth generation. It should be mentioned that few hybridists of delphiniums go this far, usually selecting the best plant from the second generation and crossing it with the desirable grandparent.

Line Breeding

Line breeding is another approach which can occasionally lead to a seed strain where a particular feature, usually colour, is fixed. The course of action is simple but it does demand patience as several years are required if you are to see satisfactory results. Results can be disappointing, but, on the other hand, with luck some remarkably good seedlings do occur.

As an example, take two seedling plants from any cross, both of which have a similar colour and perhaps also a similar habit of growth. Cross both selected seedlings and sow the seed, and in the following year select the best two seedlings which have similar colour, cross these two and again sow the seed. The following year select the best two once more and cross these. This process can of course be repeated indefinitely, and it often happens that the further this is carried out the more the progeny become fixed until it is possible that open-pollinated seed, after several generations of crossing, will yield a high percentage of plants similar to each other both in colour and form. Nothing, however, is certain and it would be misleading to give the impression that any line of hybridisation will automatically lead to success. Chance and luck so often play a part, but with any form of breeding the progeny produced will always be far superior to that which results from merely using seed from open-pollinated plants.

Making the Cross

The actual process of making the cross is simplicity itself. Pollen is contained in the anthers of each floret. If these are allowed to develop no cross is possible, for the pollen produced fertilises the stigma of the same floret and eventually sets seed. Hence the expressions 'self-pollinated' or 'open-pollinated'. To prevent this from happening a selected

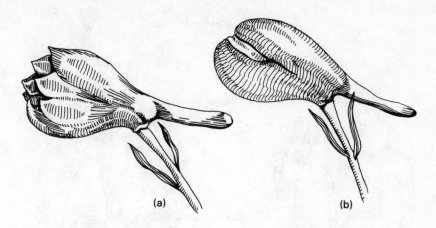

(a) This is the perfect time to tease open the floret and remove the anthers by emasculation. (b) This floret is not yet opened enough for emasculation.

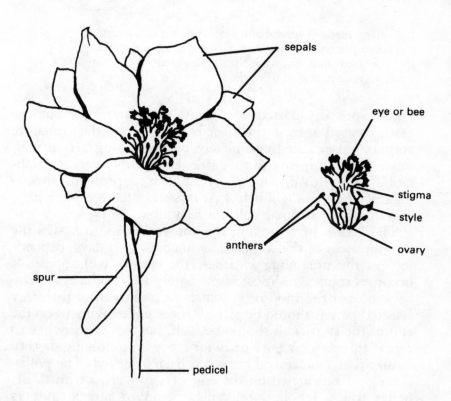

A delphinium floret with its parts named.

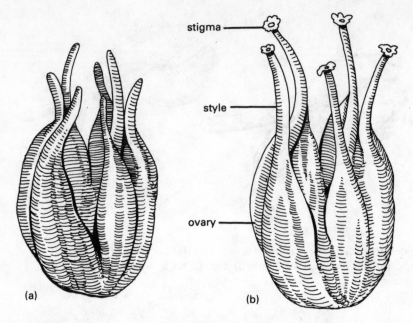

(a) Enlargement of reproductive organs after emasculation
has taken place some two days earlier. (b) About four days
from emasculation, showing the development of the stigma
ready to receive pollen from the male part of the plant.

floret from any part of the plant, even laterals, should be
gently teased open in the loose bud stage, and the immature
anthers emasculated completely by a pinching action with
fingers and thumb. (Some gardeners use tweezers to facilitate this removal, and if eyesight is a problem then a
magnifying glass will help.) At this stage the receptive part,
known as the stigma, will not be visible.

The action of removing the anthers seems to hasten the
development of the stigma, and in about four days, depending on the prevailing weather, the stigma will appear. It
becomes receptive almost immediately and produces a sticky
substance at the mouth on which the pollen from the other
selected parent should be placed. If the pollen remains on the
end of the stigma all should be well, but it is worthwhile to
repeat this process once or twice more on following days to
ensure that a successful cross has been achieved. The pollen
can either be carried on the end of a soft artist's brush or,
better still, a whole floret can be removed and the anthers
gently rubbed on the receptive stigma. Again, a magnifying
glass can be useful.

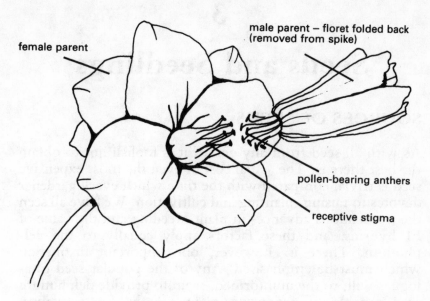

female parent

male parent – floret folded back
(removed from spike)

pollen-bearing anthers

receptive stigma

Making the cross.

There is no need to cover the floret with any protection against insects or bees, but, if birds are a problem, it can be worthwhile to tie a small muslin bag around the floret. In some districts finches do seem to regard delphinium seed as a delicacy, and they always seem to attack the hybridised seed.

You can tell after a few weeks whether the cross has been successful or not, for the pods will swell and in due time will ripen to a brown colour. Just before the pods crack it is wise to remove them and place them in an open envelope where, after a few days, the seed can be easily separated. One sure sign that the cross has failed is a twisting of the ends of the pods, which will, on examination, reveal empty cases. Once it is ripe and dry the seed is best stored in a low temperature to preserve viability. An easy way is to place the seed container in your refrigerator – but not the freezer compartment.

3

Seeds and Seedlings

SOURCES OF SEEDS

As with all seed from any genus, it is foolish not to obtain
the best there is. The actual cost of even the most expensive
seed is trivial compared with the time which every gardener
devotes to raising, planting and cultivation. We have all seen
the tremendous advances in plant breeding and the value of
F1 hybrids, and these factors apply equally to the delphinium. There is, however, one important distinction
which must be emphasised. Any of the popular seed catalogues will, to the uninformed, seem to provide delphinium
seed capable of producing plants of the finest quality.
However, it is vital to obtain seed from a specialist source,
and preferably seed from hand crosses, if you are not to be
disappointed (*see* page 140 for addresses of sources).

There is another problem in purchasing delphinium seed,
either through the post or from shops or garden centres, and
that is one of viability. To germinate effectively delphinium
seed must either be sown within a few days from harvesting,
or it must be properly stored in very cool conditions. Foil
packaging helps to a limited extent, but it is no real substitute
for the ideal environment.

STORING

Unfortunately, delphinium seed has the reputation of being
difficult to germinate, but so often the lack of success is due
to the purchase of seed which has not been properly stored.
Take, for example, seed purchased through the post from a
reliable seedsman. It may well happen that in the course of
transit the postman has placed his sack of letters against or
near to a source of heat such as a radiator. Worse still (and
this is frequently the case in garden centres), the seed may
be displayed in racks under a glass roof, and therefore subject
to extremely high temperatures. In shops central heating may
push temperatures up enough to affect germination.

To emphasise this very important aspect of storage let us take a look at how nature stores delphinium seed. The majority of species delphiniums grow in the mountainous regions of the world. Pollination takes place in the warmest, even hottest, part of the season, but the viable seed is not released from the ripened pods until late autumn when only a few will germinate, distributed by wind or birds. The majority will lie dormant in rapidly falling temperatures and remain in freezing conditions throughout the winter. With the warmer days of the following spring the seed will germinate and the tiny seedlings which germinated the previous autumn will also reappear. This explains why the ability to germinate cultivated delphinium seed decreases rapidly in inverse proportion to the rise in the temperature of the stored seed.

AUTUMN SEED SOWING

Germination

Freshly-ripened seed sown within a few days of harvesting will give the correct conditions. Germination takes place quickly, often in ten days, and this is one of the factors which prompts many amateurs to prefer autumn sowing to sowing in the spring. Autumn sowing does, however, have its disadvantages – a rather more careful approach is required and the use of a glasshouse is really desirable.

The freshly-harvested seed is usually ready by the end of August or early September in Britain, but there will be a delay of several weeks if the seed is being purchased. Seed is sown in standard trays which are placed in cool conditions. The heat in a glasshouse is far too much, as autumn sun can rocket temperatures up to 100°F (38°C) or more. A site against a north-facing wall or even a dense shrub is ideal, but you should at all costs avoid direct sunlight. It follows that protection from animals, birds and excessive rain must be taken and a sheet of glass will provide the answer.

Transplanting

Once the seed has germinated the container may be moved to a lighter position but still away from full sunlight, the dappled shade of a shrub being ideal. After about five to six

31

weeks the young seedlings will have grown sufficiently to be transplanted – ideally into 3in (7.5cm) pots – although a tray considerably deeper than a standard seed tray may be used. It is after this stage, usually around the middle to end of October, that a glass structure is useful. For ease of dealing with the pricked-out seedlings a glasshouse scores over a cold frame. The young seedlings can now tolerate the much reduced heat from the sun and the pots should be placed in the lightest part of the house, and even a modest amount of heat may be given to keep temperatures around 50°F (10°C), especially at night. Growth will continue until around December when the light factor will induce a gradual dormancy and the foliage will wither away. When they are well grown it is possible to move on to 5in (12.5cm) pots those most advanced plants before dormancy takes place. Do not be alarmed by this dying back process, and at all costs do not repeat my foolish action when I first began to grow delphiniums: I mistakenly thought that the plants had suc-cumbed to some trouble or disease and threw the contents of the pots on to a compost heap, only to find the following spring fresh growths appearing on many which had survived in spite of my rough treatment!

Environment

Unlike many greenhouse plants, such as overwintering zonal pelargoniums which require almost dry compost, the dor-mant delphiniums need a moist, but not saturated, compost at all times. Temperature from December until the end of January is relatively unimportant, and the normal conditions prevailing in the average house are quite in order. Even an unheated environment is perfectly satisfactory. With the lengthening hours of daylight at the beginning of February it is an advantage to apply a modest amount of artificial heat, but again a cold house will still be adequate, although the plants will break dormancy a few weeks later.

Further Growth and Planting Out

Whichever method is followed a minor miracle occurs. From soil level in the pots sturdy shoots will appear and a liquid feed when watering will do much to build up the plants. How has this happened? Even tiny seedlings no more than 1in (2.5cm) high will, when they die down, produce

A seedling at the correct stage for planting out into a
permanent site in the garden.

minuscule dormant eyes or buds below ground level, and it
is these which sprout into growth. Of course, the larger the
seedling at the dying back stage, the larger the eye, and
consequently the larger the shoot. This is one reason why
modest heat can be of assistance in procuring sizeable
plants.

By the end of March all the seedlings will benefit from a
move to 5in (12.5cm) pots and after a short period of
hardening off, which need not be so thorough as it might be
with other, more tender plants, they can be planted out in
their flowering positions, where they will bloom at the
normal time of June to July. This is the *advantage* of autumn
sowing – when grown well, such seedlings can produce
spikes of bloom in just ten months from sowing, and these
can be as fully developed as a mature plant thus saving the
gardener a whole season of growth.

33

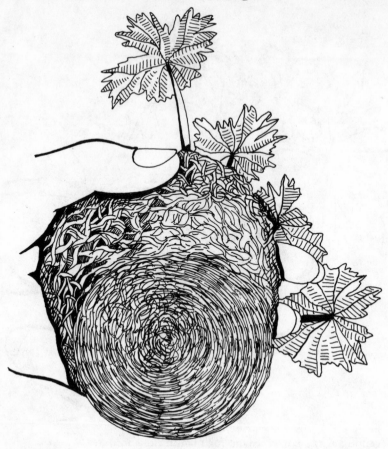

A seedling which has become pot-bound and has passed the stage when it should be planted out.

SPRING SEED SOWING

Germination

Those who have at their disposal a glasshouse can make a start by sowing seed at the end of February if a modest amount of heat can be given. The ideal temperature for germinating delphinium seed needs to be stressed as many failures occur because too much heat is given. The seed of tender plants, such as tomatoes or dahlias, requires relatively high temperatures to germinate and grow satisfactorily, but the opposite is true of the delphinium. A certain way to fail is to place the seed container in a propagating case or close to a source of heat. The most appropriate average temperature around 50°F (10°C), although a few degrees either side is no cause for alarm, so it is vital to place the pot or seed tray in a position in the glasshouse or frame that keeps it well away from any direct sunlight – under staging or shelving is ideal.

In the case of a frame, the use of netting on sunny days is advised, but it is better still to make sure that the frame is placed in such a position that the sun never strikes the glass. If you don't have the use of a glass structure a cheap but effective substitute can be a wooden box with a sheet of polythene stretched over the top. Sowing in such a device is best delayed for a few weeks until early March, and again, you will need to site the box away from direct sunlight. Spring-sown seed will take longer to germinate than autumn-sown seed – providing it has been properly stored in a low enough temperature (such as that found in an ordinary refrigerator), germination will take from three to five weeks.

'Chitting'

A novel way of germinating delphinium seed practised by some enthusiasts is to 'chit' it before sowing. This is a simple process that is worth trying and consists of placing the seed on a damp paper kitchen towel, which in turn is placed in a vessel containing water – in this way, capillary action keeps the towel moist. Modest heat is given, perhaps by putting the towel near a radiator, and once the seed has sprouted it is sown in the ordinary way.

Conditions

Whatever method you use – autumn or spring sowing – the depth at which the seed is covered is infinitely more important than the compost used. It cannot be stressed too much that failure to germinate delphinium seed can arise from too much heat, and now I must also stress that your seed should be covered with only a trace of compost, as deep sowing will never result in success. When you are covering the seed, if one or two remain on the surface then this is to be preferred to putting them in too deep.

Finally, the third factor to aid good germination is moisture context. It is difficult to overwater delphiniums, and the compost should never be allowed to dry out at any stage if successful germination is to be the result. It follows from this observation that an ideal sowing medium is one which retains moisture but allows excessive water to filter away. To this end, modern peat composts are easily improved for delphinium seed sowing by the addition of up to 50 per cent coarse sand, vermiculite or perlite, plus additional lime to help flocuation. (I confess that I personally have a preference for a seed compost based on the John Innes formula, but I am ready to admit that to find a reliable source of these composts is another matter.) There is a proprietary brand of compost based on vermiculite which is very satisfactory. This has the high moisture properties of the vermiculite, and at the same time allows masses of air to the seed. The addition of sufficient plant foods to last until the pricking-out stage leads me to a hunch that this particular compost could be said to be ideal – this is hardly surprising, for it is marketed by a leading specialist delphinium nursery.

So, the process of germination is straightforward and success is assured, providing you follow the guidelines:

1.   Fresh or properly stored seed must be used.
2.   The merest trace of compost is used to cover the seed.
3.   The compost should never be allowed to dry out.
4.   The temperature should never be allowed to rise much in excess of 50°F (10°C).

One final tip: do not get caught out by forgetting the all-important factor of not subjecting the seed to high temperatures, even for a few minutes. Keep it in the refrigerator until you are ready for sowing. It is all too easy to forget this vital consideration, and put the seed envelope on a radiator shelf or a sunny window-sill.

CULTIVATION OF SEEDLINGS

Named cultivars may sensibly be sited in a permanent position in well-prepared soil, and they may remain there, undisturbed, for many years. However, the same treatment should not be given to a plant raised from seed. Until a seedling flowers you will not know how good a plant it will be, or, indeed, if it will be worth keeping at all, and it follows that to plant a seedling in a permanent position could easily lead to disappointment. It is far better to choose a site away from the ornamental garden, and allocating a row or two in a vegetable plot is probably ideal.

A Mini Trial for Better Selection

There is no need to reserve a large area of land for the purposes of assessing the merits of a batch of delphiniums from seed. The average packet of commercial seed will produce around 100 plants and these may be planted 6in (15cm) apart each way. These planting distances are sufficient in order to ascertain the quality of each seedling, and a strip of land around 18in × 15ft (45cm × 5m) is all that will be required.

This intensive cultivation does mean that you will need to feed the seedlings at all times, but manures or fertilisers which have long-term effects are not needed as the plants will not occupy the land for longer than one year. Certain generalisations have to be made about feeding, as the fertility and type of soil varies so much from area to area and, indeed, throughout the world, and I am basing my feeding programme on my own experiences on fairly fertile and exceedingly well-drained flinty loam in Buckinghamshire.

Preparation

Delphiniums resent being planted in loose soils, and it is for this reason that any digging or cultivation of the land earmarked for the trial should be carried out at least three months before planting. Even on impermeable clay this important aspect should not be ignored, while on sandy soil the time needed for it to restabilise may well be longer. Whatever the nature of the land, it is important to add as a top dressing a general fertiliser (in generous proportions at the maximum dose recommended), and to hoe this into the top 2 or 3in (5–7·5cm) only – never deeper. Unlike many other herbaceous plants, the root structure of the delphinium consists of a mass of fine hair-like feeding roots, most of which don't penetrate the ground deeper than about 12in (30cm) throughout the life of the plant. It follows, therefore, that to place fertilisers or manures at a greater depth will simply be a wasted effort.

Planting and Cultivation

Choose a day when the soil surface is reasonably dry for the planting, and then just make a hole with a trowel, a shade deeper than the root ball or pot size, and plant firmly – I really mean firmly, and finger or hand pressure will be insufficient. The foot must be used fearlessly around the young plant to consolidate the soil. A leading professional authority adds weight to this recommendation by stating that 'more delphiniums are lost and die through loose planting than all other causes put together'.

The actual date of planting will depend on plant availability. Those raised from an autumn sowing will be ready in early March, whereas a spring sowing will produce plants of sufficient size for planting towards the end of June or beginning of July. This is also the time when young seedlings are usually available from commercial sources.

Whatever the planting date the cultivation afterwards is the same, and the most important routine to follow is to ensure that at no time is there a lack of abundant moisture in the soil. Delphiniums revel in soil which has a high water table, and consume vast quantities during their prodigious growing period. It is almost impossible to overwater the growing plant and, if in doubt, always add artificial watering during dry periods. Remember also that with artifical watering some leaching of plant foods will take place, and periodic dressings of fertilisers at six-weekly intervals will be necessary if the plants are to give of their best.

The aim with this trial of seedlings is to build up a batch of plants which will astonish you with their luxuriant growth if you feed and water really generously, and you will find that the spikes on the plants from an autumn sowing can quickly be equal to those of an established plant and of exhibition size. Now this is an important factor when the time comes to assess the plants, for you will have spikes of a representative size on which you can base an objective judgement. Spikes from an impoverished soil, on the other hand, will never give a true indication of their potential.

Growth

With an autumn sowing the first plants will begin to lengthen and show the first colour on the bottom florets from mid to late June, depending on locality and season. If you have selected seed from the right sources, or you have used your own hybridised seed, I can promise you the thrill of a lifetime spread over a period of about a month. Every day a new colour will appear as fresh florets open, and the

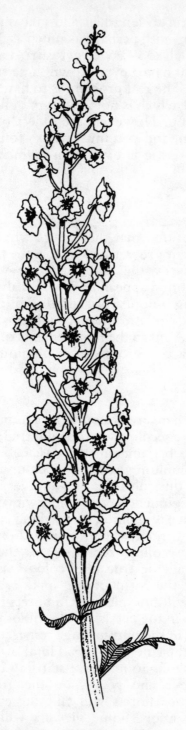

The ideal shape and form of a delphinium spike.

spikes will begin to lengthen and take shape in a beautiful spiral of colour, with perhaps as much as 3½ft (1·8m) length of bloom. It is all too easy to get carried away at this stage, especially if you have never grown these superb plants from specialist seed. The real problem is to harden your heart and reject any plant which is not perfect in build, for they will all look outstanding. However, the object of this mini trial is one of selection, and you must banish to the compost heap, as soon as flowering is over, those which are obviously of poor quality.

Selection

It must be admitted that the factors which the enthusiastic specialist amateur grower looks for in the perfect delphinium are not necessarily the same as those which the average gardener might find appealing. There is always an element of a cult following among specialists of all types of flowering plants and the dogmatic approach which so often is a feature is perhaps irrelevant to the requirements of the gardener who just wants attractive groups of delphiniums in his borders.

Colour

Nevertheless, there are bound to be a number of undesirable features in some seedlings in the mini trial which may not be obvious to the beginner in this fascinating and rewarding aspect of delphinium growing. Colour is the one feature which is most difficult to assess, and yet it is the subject on which most beginners have definite views. I can best illustrate the variance of opinion by recalling comments made by visitors to my garden when I have had on view as many as three hundred seedlings blooming for the first time. Some will pick out all the true blue colours as their favourites, irrespective of the form of the spike which may be very poor. Others will find pleasure in florets having a combination of colours in the petals, while still others seem to prefer strong colours in the purple range, especially when there is a contrasting light-coloured eye. Floral arrangers will select those spikes which do not have startling contrasts of colour between the eye and petals, on the grounds that in an arrangement such florets will take the eye away from the general composition. Some viewers will go into raptures over the dusky-pink range, whereas others will regard such shades with some genuine distaste. The silvery effect on some florets will usually be praised, and the pure whites are always admired.

So it seems that colour is one aspect that must be left to the raiser and his or her own particular fancy. However, before leaving this somewhat controversial subject I feel I must mention something which has only recently come to my attention – the question of colour blindness. If you are among this group, even if only partially so, then I do recommend you seek the opinion of those who are not. For many years I have been puzzled as to why some particular combinations of colours, which have been hideous to my eye, have been selected time and time again by certain individuals. The explanation came when I learned that they were colour blind. In the ordinary way this would not matter at all, but it would assume importance in the event of any favoured seedling being submitted to the Royal Horticultural Society for an award.

Constitution

Robustness is universally regarded by many experts as the single most important factor in assessing the quality of a delphinium. We can eliminate some seedlings from the trial during the first year by rejecting any which fracture during summer storms. Unfortunately, these storms too often coincide with the season during which the delphiniums are at their peak. It is no use retaining these seedlings however desirable they may be in other respects, for such a weakness will be exposed year after year. The other aspect of constitution concerns the true perennial characteristics of the plant. Clearly, this quality will only become apparent over a period of years, and in some cases you will find that the odd plant will not survive even to the following year.

Florets and Shape

The actual shape of individual florets can vary enormously, as can their placement on the stem. Be on the lookout for any plants which produce florets at irregular intervals – such a fault will always be repeated through the years. Sometimes the eye of the plant will not be well defined, and the pigment can also smear or smudge on to the actual petals. The manner in which pedicels are carried on the stem can cause

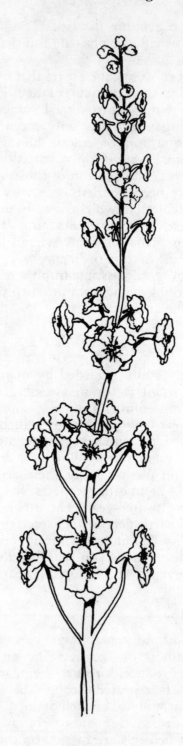

'Bunching'.

Florets hanging down – 'shy'.

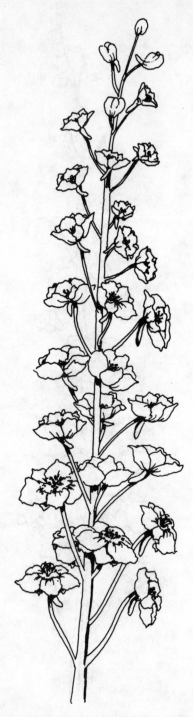

Florets pointing upwards – 'proud'.

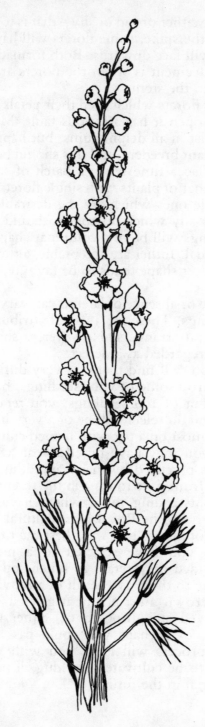

Bottom florets shedding petals before the top ones are open.

the florets to be either proud or shy – that is to say, when you are looking at the spike, some florets will hang downwards whilst others will face upwards. Both formations are faulty. The perfect placement is when the florets are virtually at a vertical plane to the stem.

If a plant has florets which shed their petals before the top-most ones are open it has a serious fault. Many years ago, this used to exist in all delphiniums, but happily it has been corrected by plant breeders, and this should be your aim too.

There was also a time when a batch of seedlings would produce a number of plants with single florets, as opposed to the semi-double ones which are the desirable ones. This is rare today, but any which do appear should be discarded.

Some seedlings will be of a columnar shape whilst others will be pyramidal. Either are acceptable, although it must be said that the latter shape tends to be favoured in delphinium circles.

The presence or absence of laterals can vary markedly on a batch of seedlings. These are a useful attribute, for they are coveted by floral arrangers. However, a shortage of them should not be regarded as a defect.

I am sure you will find that it is very difficult to be bold enough to destroy some of your seedlings, but you must be objective. If, out of 100 seedlings, you retain only a few, those which you do select will be of a very high quality and may well be almost on a par with named cultivars. It is even possible that you may have raised a real 'winner', for this form of trial is practised by many an enthusiastic amateur. Growers have from time to time in the recent past produced seedlings of outstanding merit which have eventually re-ceived awards from the Royal Horticultural Society.

When the blooms are past their best the time has come to remove those you have selected to a more permanent position. Provided they retain as much soil as possible no harm will come to them as a result of a move, but watering the replanted crown must not be neglected. Those rejected are also removed and disposed of, either by way of the compost heap, or perhaps you could pass the best on to friends. This process will leave you with your mini trial ground ready to be cultivated and dug, if necessary, ready for a further trial in the future.

4

Vegetative Propagation

Whilst it *is* possible to increase a delphinium by splitting the crown of an established plant, in much the same way as with many other perennial plants, this method is far from satisfactory. Unlike, for example, a Michaelmas Daisy (perennial aster) which can be teased apart quite easily into separate pieces, the root structure of a delphinium consists of a hard crown which requires the use of a very sharp knife in order to divide it into sections. The wound created is very prone to 'bleeding', and even a dressing of sulphur or other fungicides does little to heal the wound or prevent the entry of diseases. Even if you are successful in this, the divided pieces seldom perform well.

CUTTINGS

Happily delphiniums may be propagated vegetatively by taking cuttings. They are not as easy as, for example, a chrysanthemum, but, as long as a few basic rules are followed, success is guaranteed.

The easiest way to facilitate the removal of immature shoots is to dig up the crown of a plant in late January or early February, and place it into a container surrounded by soil or damp peat. Given the protection of glass, in the form of a frame or a glasshouse, the crown will produce shoots within a few weeks. As soon as the most forward shoots are around 2–3in (5–7·5cm) high they should be severed from the crown. Care is needed in this operation and a really sharp knife is required – the best thing to use is one of the many craft tools available with disposable blades from model shops and some hardware stores. The cut must be made close to the crown so that a minute part of the actual crown itself is removed with the cutting. Any ragged pieces or snags should be trimmed back. Before inserting the cutting into the rooting media, examine the cut end – it should be solid and whitish in colour. Any which appear hollow have been severed too far away from the base and, whilst they *may*

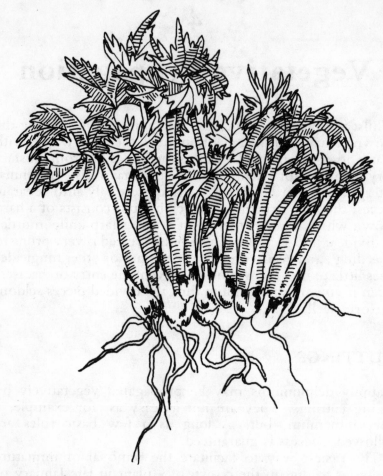

The lifted crown of a mature plant at the correct stage to
secure cuttings.

root, such cuttings seldom form a crown and will eventually
die.

Another method of securing cuttings is to take them *in situ*.
This is known as 'scrabbling'. The *Oxford Dictionary* describes
this word as 'to scrawl, scratch, grope or scramble about',
and this is exactly the process. I confess that it is a process
which, with advancing years, I am unhappy to contemplate,
but I must have taken many hundreds of cuttings this way
when younger. It simply means facing a cold late February
or March day (or even early April in a late season), getting
down on all fours and gently removing the soil from around
the crown of the plant until the shoots are revealed where

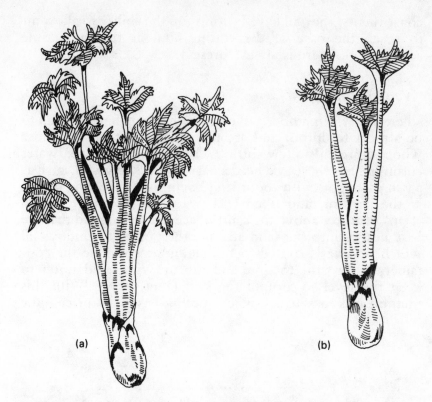

(a) The cutting, having been removed with a sharp blade, but not yet prepared. (b) The same cutting being prepared for insertion in rooting media, showing fairly ruthless removal of leaves.

they join the crown. One successful grower of my acquaintance achieves this by using the jet of a hose to wash away the soil. It must be carefully carried out, for it is all too easy to damage surrounding tissue which contains further embryo shoots. The shoots are removed in a similar way to those already described on the crown of the plant which has been dug up, and further visits can be made as more shoots develop over a period of several weeks. A danger with this method is the potential damage to the crown, and it is prudent to dress the wound made with a proprietary fungicide to seal the cut and prevent disease.

Rooting

Many specialists have their own pet formulas for the composts they use to root cuttings. When you examine the constituents, they all have in common the ability to allow air to reach the base of the cutting, but at the same time adequate moisture is always present.

'Water Cuttings'

There are two methods which over the years have proved to be almost foolproof and are particularly suitable for those who require only a few cuttings. By far the easiest are 'water cuttings'. For these you need a narrow-necked vessel, such as a fish paste pot, with about 1in (2.5cm) of coarse sand or grit in the bottom, and filled with water so that there is ½in (1cm) of water above the sand. Place the cuttings so that the base nestles into the sand and site the pot on a window-sill which is never exposed to full sunlight. Examine the containers from time to time and top up with tepid water to keep the level to around the ½in (1cm) mark. With this method it is easy to see when rooting has taken place – the

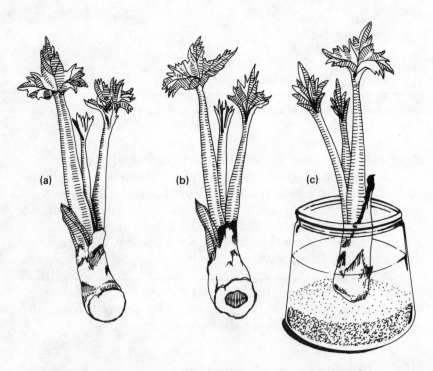

(a) A good cutting showing a solid base. (b) A poor cutting showing a hollow stem at the base. (c) An easy method of rooting a cutting.

shoots may be lifted out of the water and examined, and replaced if no roots are present. Rooting usually occurs within a period of three to five weeks and potting-up may then be carried out in traditional composts. It is easy to appreciate the convenience of such a method, for one pot, suitably labelled, may be used for one cultivar and cuttings may be added as and when they become available over a period of several weeks.

Saturated Perlite

A variation on this method, perhaps more suitable for those with a glasshouse and who require rather more cuttings, is to take a half pot or a seed tray and fill it with perlite. This is in turn placed into a tray of water (a cat-litter tray, available at pet shops, is ideal). The saturated perlite helps the cuttings, which are inserted to a depth of about 1in (2.5cm), to remain upright, and, as with water cuttings, they may be removed to see if rooting has taken place. Again, be careful to place the tray in a position away from the direct rays of the sun, or provide shading. Top up the water as and when necessary.

Sharp Sand

The traditional method of rooting a cutting, which was practised almost universally until comparatively recently, still has some advantages, especially for those with little time at their disposal since it avoids the potting-up stage. A John Innes-type potting compost should be used to fill a 4in (10cm) pot, and a depression some 1in (2.5cm) deep by 1in (2.5cm) wide should be made in the centre, filled with very sharp sand, and the cutting inserted. A thorough watering should be given, which is best achieved by standing the pot in water and allowing capillary action to saturate the contents, thereby avoiding wet foliage. A frame, or box covered with glass or clear plastic, is essential, for at no time should the cuttings be subjected to temperatures in excess of around 55°F (13°C). Site the frame or box against a north-facing wall. Rooting will be hastened if some protection from frost can be given. This is ideally achieved by using a second frame light, which has the same insulating effect as domestic double glazing. Alternatively, a covering of an old bedding blanket may be used at night when frosts are at their sharpest – this must be removed during hours of daylight.

It is fairly obvious that with this method the roots, as they form in the sand, penetrate into the soil compost and continue to grow. At the same time, as growth becomes advanced, air may be admitted by raising the glass gradually, so that after about eight weeks the rooted cuttings have become young plants already hardened off and ready for planting out.

Mist Propagation

If, as is perhaps possible, you are using the fairly modern method of rooting cuttings, on a wide range of plants there would seem to be potential advantages in trying mist propagation. Unfortunately, all attempts with delphiniums have so far proved disasterous. The majority of cuttings placed in the mist soon rot, and the percentage which survive long enough to form roots has been extremely small.

Laboratory Methods

Some experiments have been conducted with delphiniums using micro-propagation techniques, which have been so successful with certain other genera. To the best of my knowledge, however, there have not been any recorded cases where this method of propagation has been used successfully with delphiniums.

Eye Cuttings

The final method of securing cuttings by using eyes has been left until last, because it would be misleading to give the impression that it is easy to accomplish. It can, however, be a very useful method to know.

After flowering, all top growth should be removed to ground level and the plants involved should be given a thorough watering. After some three weeks or so the crown of the plant should be removed from the ground, and all soil should be washed completely from the stool. On examination the crown will reveal a number of embryo shoots, or buds or eyes, as they are known, varying from match-head to thumb-nail size. In shape they look very similar to a dormant crocus bulb. Any which are larger than ¼in (0.5cm) in diameter are removed in the same way as orthodox cuttings, close to the crown. Using a compost

Lifted crown in August, showing old flowering stems and
dormant eyes.

containing an abundance of drainage material such as sharp
sand, perlite or vermiculite, the tiny eyes should be inserted
at a depth roughly equivalent to their size so that the top is
just below the compost level. As mildew spores can be
present a watering with a fungicide should be given. The
container, pot or seed tray, should then be placed in a cold
frame, or a box with a sheet of glass, in a position away from
direct sunlight. As temperatures at this time of year are
usually above 60°F (15°C), the use of a hormone rooting
powder will without doubt assist in the rooting process and
one containing a fungicide is to be recommended.

If all goes well, rooting will take place from three to five
weeks, but as these tiny plants are vulnerable they require
careful handling. Each should be potted up separately into a
3in (7.5cm) pot, and returned to a glass-protected environment for a further two to three weeks, by which time the
most forward may be ready for planting out. In a late season,
however, it often happens that these eye cuttings will not
have made sufficient growth and are best left in the pots until
the following year. They will of course die back, but tiny
embryo eyes will have formed, which will emerge the
following spring and can be safely planted out into their
flowering positions.

It must be admitted that many who have tried this method
have not achieved a high percentage of success, while others
have not been troubled with any problems. It does have the

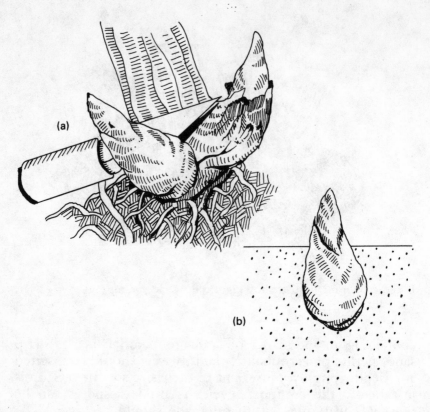

(a) The correct method of removing the eye. (b) The right depth is important.

advantage, especially with a new and promising seedling, of enabling you to obtain a large quantity of plants quickly. It is quite possible to secure as many as fifty plants from a mature stool, and even with a maiden plant I have taken on several occasions around twenty eyes, of which 75 per cent produced strong young plants.

Hygiene and Hormone Rooting

It is possible to transmit virus diseases from one cutting to another by the knife, and it is therefore prudent to sterilise the blade by dipping it into a solution of any proprietary brand of steriliser. (One product which is easily obtainable is 'Milton', which should be diluted according to the instructions.)

There is some controversy over the use of rooting compounds. I personally feel that for the purposes of the delphinium grower they are unnecessary, for there is evidence

54

that they do not release the hormones in temperatures below 60°F (15°C) Since our aim is to achieve an average temperature of around 55°F (13°C), they would seem to be inoperative. However, some compounds do also contain a fungicide, so it is true that no harm can be caused by their use, and they may be of benefit.

Potting Composts

Ideally the cutting should be potted up, as soon as roots have formed, into a compost similar to that recommended for seed-raised plants (*see* Chapter 3). As soon as the pots are well filled with roots, but before they become pot-bound, they can be planted out into their permanent position. The soil preparation will differ considerably from the methods carried out for the site which occupied the mini trial of seed-sown plants.

SOIL PREPARATION

The life-span of a modern cultivar does vary. Some may be comparatively short-lived and may need replacing after some three years or so, but the vast majority are capable of producing vigorous spikes for many years. I have had numerous plants which have continued for as long as thirteen years to bloom satisfactorily, and it follows that every gardener should prepare his soil with long-term considerations in mind.

It is pointless to be dogmatic about the steps you should take to prepare the soil – the variation is so wide that all growers will need to make adjustments to the recommendations given in light of their own circumstances. What is certain is the fact that delphiniums will grow satisfactorily in a wide range of soils. A survey conducted by the Delphinium Society some years ago revealed that successful growers gardened on soil ranging from low to high pH values, from chalk to sand, and from loam to clay. One successful exhibitor even called his soil 'London dirt'.

The feeding roots of the delphinium do not extend much more than 12in (30cm) below soil level and, providing drainage is adequate, there is little point in cultivating the soil to a greater depth. If you are unfortunate enough to garden on a very sticky clay then perhaps a deeper cultivation may be necessary in order to provide drainage, but for most gardens a thorough improvement in soil texture for about 12in (30cm) will repay handsomely the labour involved. Make no mistake – the delphinium is a gross feeder and will revel in a soil which contains an abundance of moisture. For this reason a site away from tree, hedge or shrub roots is to be preferred, although the competition of the roots of other perennial plants can be tolerated.

As much organic matter as possible should be added to the soil well in advance of planting time. Animal manures are superb, but spent mushroom compost is a very good alternative and properly-made garden compost is also extremely satisfactory. A word of caution is needed concerning peat. Peat-based products are virtually devoid of plant nutrients and are very acid, and there is thus the real danger of 'locking-up' the vital elements of soil fertility. To counteract the effect, some lime should be added, as well as some nitrogen fertilisers, when incorporating the peat into the soil.

In any event it pays to give the young delphinium plants a good start and to this end the long-term fertilisers usually based on organic materials are to be preferred. Coarse ground bone-meal is ideal, for it contains phosphates which encourage the formation of a good root structure. A little nitrogen is also present, but this can be supplemented by the use of hoof and horn-meal, which, if coarsely ground, will provide a steady supply of nitrogen over several years.

If you want to take soil fertility seriously, then you can have an analysis provided by your local council at a modest cost. This will certainly take the guesswork out of soil preparation. For example, one leading grower who had added considerable quantities of bone-meal to his soil over the years discovered, on receiving his soil report, that the sample sent for analysis contained an excess of phosphates. In this case the addition of any fertiliser containing this element would be pointless and perhaps even harmful.

5

Cultivation

Delphiniums are some of the first of the hardy perennials to show signs of growth in the early spring. Indeed, in some years young shoots will be observed breaking through the soil in early February in the south of Britain. Since the root structure of the delphinium is in the top 12in (30cm) of soil, it is a mistake to cultivate the soil too deeply, for this disturbance will cause damage to the feeding roots. The hoe is the tool to use rather than the border fork.

Even with plants which are merely required for garden adornment a dressing of a general fertiliser is desirable at this stage of breaking through. For exhibition purposes it is essential and the highest rate recommended on the packet should be given.

THINNING

When the shoots are around 5–6in (13–15cm) high some thinning will almost certainly be required for garden display – for exhibition it will be vital. This operation makes sense for it has the same effect as, for example, the pruning of roses or the stopping and disbudding of dahlias or chrysan-themums. On a one-year-old plant it is sensible to reduce the number of shoots to no more than three, and even on a vigorous, established plant seven should be regarded as the maximum. This simple process of cutting out unwanted shoots at ground level will not only improve materially the quality of the remaining spikes, but will also lay a foundation for the future well-being of the plant during its lifetime.

STAKING

Most modern cultivars will require some form of support. This can be a chore, and in the case of the unthinned plant, which can produce twenty or more spikes, it is almost impossible to attend to satisfactorily. However, if you are dealing with a properly thinned plant with seven spikes or less the problem is somewhat easier. The individual spikes will not be as tall, and the stems will also become harder as more sun and air are admitted, so there will be less chance of fracture.

There was a time when some enthusiasts tied one spike to a cane from the bottom to the top. This cannot be recommended, on aesthetic grounds alone, and it is hardly necessary, even with the tallest of modern cultivars. If, however, your garden is on a hilly, windswept site then your choice of plants should be made from the wide range now available of those which seldom exceed 4ft (120cm) in height. Indeed, the giant plants often sought after by the exhibitor really have no place for garden adornment and are certainly out of character, especially with the ever-decreasing size of gardens attached to modern housing developments.

The most favoured method of supporting an established plant is to use three canes in the form of a triangle and to place them in the ground so that they are splayed out at an angle away from the stems with roughly 3ft (90cm) of cane protruding. This enables the plants to sway in the wind without breakage as ties are added as the plant grows. With very tall plants perhaps three loops will be required, although I have found two are usually sufficient. Another method sometimes adopted, which requires more labour, is to use one cane per shoot and to make two ties as the plant grows. Great care must be taken with the top tie – if it is too tight the plant will not be able to sway in windy weather and, should a summer storm arise during the peak flowering period, a whiplash effect can be created so that the spike, heavy with water, snaps at the tie. A loose tie will do much to prevent this mishap.

WATERING

If an abundance of organic matter was added to the soil when it was being prepared, then in most summers this should be sufficient on most soils to provide adequate moisture. Impoverished soils or those with exceptional drainage will benefit greatly if a mulch of organic matter can be given early in the season – bark fibre is absolutely ideal.

Young plants set out in the spring will, however, require additional watering until they are established, and in real

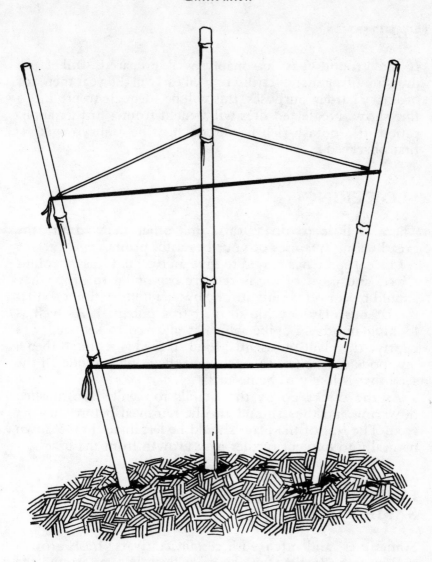

A favoured method of supporting an established plant, using
three canes in the form of a triangle.

drought conditions, which are experienced in Britain from
time to time, some artificial watering may be prudent if the
plants are to give of their best. It is vital that this artificial
watering should be continued until it reaches the soil at a
point below the root structure. This does mean leaving the
sprinkler in position for a minimum of about three hours.

FEEDING

If the ground was reasonably well prepared, and a top dressing of a general fertiliser given early in the year then, for ordinary garden purposes, this will be adequate to produce a fine show. Neglected sites will benefit from a further application of a potash-rich fertiliser when the embryo spike is first observed.

FLOWERING

There is little to do at this time other than admire the breathtaking qualities of your beautiful plants.

Once a spike has ceased to give an overall pleasant colour effect, and most of the florets are beginning to drop, they should be cut off cleanly just below the bottom floret so that the laterals may develop to their true potential. As well as looking untidy, a spike which is allowed to set seed will deprive the plant of essential food. If seed is required then a few pods can be left to ripen, and they will provide all the seed that is likely to be needed.

As the weeks go by the laterals too will have finished flowering and they should also be removed before they set seed. The rest of the plant should be left intact to die down naturally to prevent further new growth from the base.

FURTHER FLOWERING IN THE SAME YEAR

Sometimes, and often with certain cultivars, fresh growth will appear shortly after the main flush is over around the end of July. You should allow this bonus to flower and encourage it to do so by removing all old growth.

Normally, if you allowed all the plants to flower twice during the same year then the following year's display would be seriously weakened, presenting a very sorry sight of poor, undersized, spindly spikes. There is one way, however, to enjoy a breathtaking second display in the late summer or early autumn, without suffering the unhappy spectacle of a motley assortment of poor spikes the following year. You will need to be prepared for some labour, but in my opinion it is well worth it. (Note: the procedure is more practical if a bed has been devoted to delphiniums alone rather than to a mixed border.)

The secret is to have in reserve some young plants, either cuttings taken the same spring, or seedlings, also sown in the spring. These young plants should be potted up in stages until, by the end of the summer, they are in large pots – I have found that 8in (20cm) plastic ones are adequate for the final potting. In the early months of the year they are best sited in full sun, but from early June onwards a semi-shaded place is to be desired, as this will considerably decrease the need constantly to water the pots until the time comes to plant them. Do not allow these plants to flower, but keep pinching out any flower buds which appear.

Returning to the site of your main display, you must remove all growth to ground level as soon as the flowering is past its best. At the same time, a dressing must be given of a balanced fertiliser which is high in nitrogen. This should be soluble powder rather than a granular type, for the sooner this nourishment is available to the soil the better. The fertiliser should be hoed into the top few inches of soil and, unless there is likely to be heavy rain, a thorough watering of the plant should take place.

The removal of all growth, the application of the fertiliser and the warmth of the ground will stimulate the plant to send up fresh shoots in a surprisingly short time, and thinning should be carried out in the same way as for plants growing during their normal flowering period. The task of supporting the stems is made easier because the original canes will have been left in position. In some favourable summers this forced second blooming starts from mid to late September, but it can be as late as the end of October in a less auspicious season. One added bonus which often comes as a surprise is the length of the display – the second flowers will last a longer period than those delphiniums blooming at the normal time (during June and July), simply because the temperature is considerably lower in the autumn.

Colour Change

Be prepared for an astonishing change in the colour of the florets. This is so pronounced that it never ceases to intrigue me whenever I see a well-known cultivar producing a representative spike in the autumn. The difference can be so extraordinary that even the most expert enthusiast fails to recognise some cultivars, but it is very difficult to define in words the change which takes place. Colours seem more intense and pink tones often replace the blue ones. I can, however, promise you a breathtaking display which can come as quite a shock to knowledgeable gardeners who may visit you. The quality of the second blooms can be every bit as good as those which flowered months earlier. This was confirmed by a nurseryman of my acquaintance who, knowing that he was changing the site of his commercial plantation, carried out this experiment. The display of spikes which he subsequently showed at an autumn show of the Royal Horticultural Society in London caused a minor sensation.

AFTER FLOWERING

As soon as this welcome display is over, the plants should be removed, but not necessarily destroyed. Whilst it is extremely unlikely that they would ever again produce worthwhile blooms if transplanted elsewhere, they can be valuable as stock plants. Any which you would like to propagate should be replanted into a temporary site in some out-of-the-way spot, in order that they may be dug up in the following spring and cuttings taken in the ordinary way.

Before setting out the replacement plants the site should be cleared of all debris and a dressing of a fertiliser should be given. Avoid the use of a high nitrogen analysis as the aim is to encourage root formation rather than top growth. To this end a tomato fertiliser is ideal. Again, these large plants from equally large pots require firm planting, followed by a thorough watering unless heavy rainfall occurs or is forecast. If in doubt *always* water! Whilst there is some urgency to get this replanting carried out as soon as possible, it is not deserving of as much priority as would seem to be the case. There is unquestionable evidence that root formation continues well into December in Britain, even though top growth is actually dying back. The display the following year can be almost as good as the result of a late spring planting, although it is prudent to thin the shoots rather more drastically. In less vigorous plants it may be necessary to restrict the stems to one or two spikes per plant.

NORMAL TREATMENT

Those mature plants which are being retained in the ordinary way to flower again the following year require, needless to say, rather different treatment. The foliage should be left intact until the end of October or early November, when the plants can be cut down to ground level. This is important because any stumps of old stems which are left can collect water and stagnate, possibly causing rotting of the crown. Finally, always clean the soil thoroughly of all debris to discourage slugs and take action should this pest be suspected (*see* Chapter 6).

6

Pests and Diseases

SLUGS AND SNAILS

Few pests can cause damage to delphiniums, but the members of the molluscous family can become a major problem. It is essential to take steps to prevent slugs, in particular, from invading the site where delphiniums are grown – they can cause so much damage to the embryo shoots below ground that the plant may even die. At best, any shoots left will be seriously weakened and the display of spikes will be so puny that they will not justify any effort spent on cultivation.

Before suggesting an effective means of control, a brief outline of the species and life cycle of this pest will help the gardener to understand the way in which to rid the site once and for all of slugs and snails.

All slugs are both hermaphrodite and protandrous, which means in simple terms that, at certain stages in their development they have both male and female characteristics. They can lay eggs numbering as many as 300 at one time, and this prodigious breeding factor is of vital importance. If we link measures of control to coincide with the breeding period we will go some way to prevent further egg-laying.

The slug which does the most damage in gardens, often referred to by the layman as the 'keel slug', is *Arion hortensis*, which lays its eggs during May, and again in late September and early October. This slug is both a surface scavenger as well as a burrower, and it principally attacks the young dormant buds below soil level as they form. It follows that control measures should be taken in early May and again in mid-September, thus destroying this specie before it lays its eggs.

Slugs require moist conditions at all times, otherwise they will dehydrate and die. One myth that should be exploded is that they do not like gritty substances. It is not the sharpness of the grit that they object to, but the fact that large grains of any substance do not hold much in the way of moisture content – so slugs avoid such substances in view of the comparative dryness. A simple experiment can prove that slugs require a moist environment. If you place a plank of wood on the soil surface, having watered the ground beforehand, they will cling to it. If slugs are a problem, then an examination of the underside of the plank the following morning will reveal quite a catch. This is one way of trapping the pest, but there are many better methods. Still, it proves that leaving rubbish and litter about on the soil is a sure way of increasing the population of this pest.

Some years ago I was surprised to find some slug damage among my recently planted delphiniums, as I thought that I had taken sufficient measures to ensure they would not be a problem. At that time I was planting some young rooted cuttings from 3in (7.5cm) pots which had been given to me by an acquaintance. To my consternation I found the soil ball around the roots was 'alive' with tiny, newly-hatched slugs, and so the cause of the problem was revealed, for the slug-damaged plants had come from the same source. The old saying 'prevention is better than cure' is certainly true, and it also applies to plants in pots. As a routine measure I now always water the pots just before planting with a solution of aluminium sulphate at the correct rate.

Aluminium Sulphate

There are several chemicals freely available from commercial chemical suppliers which are effective in controlling slugs. Most are poisonous to other forms of life, including pets and, indeed, ourselves, and for this reason they are best avoided. Fortunately, one of the most effective is aluminium sulphate. This is a very safe chemical and in its purified form it can be bought at any chemist being effective in the treatment of mouth ulcers with its highly astringent action. It certainly has an effect on slugs and, perhaps more significant, it also dissolves slug eggs. Because of its caustic nature it needs to be handled cautiously, but as long as you are careful not to wet any foliage no harm will be caused to the plants. Indeed, a form of this chemical is used to 'blue' hydrangea plants growing in alkaline soils.

The best way to apply aluminium sulphate is in solution rather than as powder. Simply dissolve 2oz for every gallon of water (about 50g for every 4 litres) and saturate the soil around the crown of each plant, taking great care not to wet the foliage. I have found 2 pints (about 1 litre) per plant to be about the right dosage. One application made in the late autumn, another in early February, and one in May will usually be sufficient to provide effective control. If, however, the soil is really badly infested, then further applications can be given at two-monthly intervals.

As far as can be judged no damage occurs to the crown or dormant eyes of a delphinium by the use of this chemical, but I would not recommend a more highly concentrated solution just in case the caustic effect proves to be damaging. Of all the measures which you can take I regard this method of warfare on slugs to be the most efficacious because it destroys their eggs as well.

Other Methods

The more familiar method of control is by the use of pellets. Those on sale at most garden suppliers are either based on metaldehyde or, more recently, on methiocarb. The former chemical is quite definitely poisonous and it is often advocated in the older type of gardening literature where you are told to mix ground-up meta fuel with bran or tea leaves, and place heaps around the garden. This advice I strongly deprecate. It will certainly attract slugs who will consume vast quantities and some will undoubtedly be destroyed. If, however, rain falls within a few days, not only is the bait rendered useless, but many of the slugs will recover from their intake of poison. Worse still is the potential harm which can be caused to pets and wild life. Even in pelleted form I would not care to use any product based on metaldehyde for even if it is protected by a covering, as often advocated, the danger is still there.

The material now used by farmers and nurserymen to combat slugs is based on methiocarb, which is a comparatively new discovery and can be obtained in pelleted form from some garden suppliers. Without doubt the tiny bluish pellets are very effective, and even more important is the fact that once they have been consumed by a slug, no recovery will take place, even during lengthy periods of rain. They are considerably more cost-effective than metaldehyde and should, in my opinion, have completely replaced this doubtful chemical. Whilst I cannot be dogmatic on the question of safety I am informed that the ingredients in methiocarb-based pellets are not harmful to other forms of life, but I must confess that I have some doubts as I am sure that they are also lethal to earthworms. This is a very sad side-effect, if not a serious disadvantage. I can only suggest caution if you choose to use this undoubtedly effective measure.

The methods advocated by 'fringe' gardeners would fill almost a chapter, and they range from beer to orange peel traps, to nightly patrols with a torch physically to remove and destroy the slugs on the move. Circles of zinc around plants will certainly deter surface slugs from touching this metal, but do nothing for the burrowing slug, as indeed is the case for most, if not all, of these fanciful remedies. They are, in my opinion, about as effective as tying an onion around your head, or trying any of the other hilarious remedies which are supposed to relieve the common cold. In reality these ideas do nothing other than provide friends and neighbours with a good source of merriment by their very absurdity.

CATERPILLARS

I do not regard the caterpillar as a serious threat to the delphinium, although it can certainly be a nuisance if some promising spikes are attacked. In some years it makes no appearance at all and in some districts it is never seen. Why this should be the case is not known, in spite of limited research by certain enthusiasts.

The tortrix moth is usually the culprit and, as with most moths, it lays its eggs during hours of darkness and is seldom seen in daylight. Unlike butterflies, which can lay many eggs in clusters, it seems that only one or two eggs are laid at one time, and a delphinium plant will never become infested with eggs in the same way that the cabbage white butterfly can affect brassicas. This is one reason why the caterpillar does not represent a serious threat.

The tortrix moth is on the wing during May. The eggs take seven days to hatch and one certain way of detecting the caterpillar is to find an immature leaf which has been rolled up by the pest to provide a hiding place during daylight hours. These are easily discovered and handpicking will provide all the control necessary. Spraying is not needed, unless vast quantities of delphiniums are planted, for a daily visit will reveal the few plants which may be attacked. The larvae of the tortrix moth will overwinter in the host plant, one of which is the delphinium, and its favourite place is in the hollow stem when the plant has been cut down. It is important, therefore, that this cutting-down process should be at, or slightly below, ground level, so that no hollow stem is left. This action, together with the hand picking of the caterpillar already mentioned, will go a long way to preventing any serious build-up of the moth.

EELWORM

As is the case with many other flowers, if delphiniums are grown habitually in the same soil for many years, it is possible that there will be a gradual build-up of harmful organisms – hence the desirability, for example, of rotating vegetable crops. This rotation should also apply to the delphinium in order to be sure of avoiding this problem. It would be wise if you are growing them in a concentrated fashion to change the site every six years or so, but in the ordinary mixed border it is unlikely to become a problem.

Some enthusiasts have made the mistake of reserving sites for intensive planting of delphiniums, using the same plot for many years. In some cases after a long period of, perhaps, as much as ten years there has been a build-up of eelworm. This can be so serious that delphiniums cease to thrive and there really is no alternative to a complete change of site and to growing other plants which are not attacked by the eelworm peculiar to the delphinium, which is known as *Pratyenchus pratensis*.

There is no really effective way of destroying eelworm, for the high concentration of sterilising chemicals, such as formaldehyde, needed to be effective requires careful use and has the disadvantage that all forms of organisms and plant growth in the vicinity are also destroyed. This makes its use impractical in gardens where other decorative plants are grown. Moreover, as the eelworm can survive for countless years in desiccated form, there is no point in replanting an infested soil at any time in future years as the eelworm will soon regain a foothold.

You should, however, keep the potential problem of eelworm in perspective. It is extremely unlikely ever to pose a serious threat to the ordinary garden, and some enthusiasts have grown plants on the same site for a lifetime, and have never experienced any great problem with this particular pest.

MILDEW

There is absolutely no need to have mildew on delphiniums, since there are available cultivars that never suffer with this malady. A planting of these mildew-resistant cultivars will ensure that you never have the problem.

However, there are some really exquisite cultivars which are very prone to mildew, particularly among the deeper colours and especially the purples. If you cannot resist the temptation to grow these plants, which are lovely but susceptible, then you will need to be prepared to spray with a modern fungicide, in which case mildew will be only a mild problem.

Fortunately, mildew does not usually appear until after flowering. There can be some seasons, especially when delphiniums are grown in an environment of high humidity such as that found in a densely-planted garden, when some disfigurement can occur on the mature flower spike. Such sites should be avoided, but certainly this may not be possible in a garden containing a mixed planting including trees and shrubs, which is often desirable. The alternative is to use a modern systemic fungicide before mildew appears. A spray at the end of May is usually effective, and a further application a week before flowering commences may be necessary in severe cases. It is a surprising fact that even very badly affected plants are able to manufacture plump dormant eyes which flower normally the following year, and there is no evidence that mildew reduces the vigour of delphiniums.

ROT

Sometimes a plant will collapse and an examination of the crown will reveal a complete disintegration of the tissue. This malady, which rarely occurs, is often inaccurately referred to as 'black rot'. Do not be misled by this term for 'black rot' is confined to America and is a serious disease.

There are several causes of rot. More often than not the plant has lived out its useful life-span, and there is some evidence that the life of a delphinium can be shortened by poor cultivation, including the heavy use of nitrogenous fertilisers, coupled with poor drainage. Wounds created to the crown by the careless use of border forks or hoes can be so bad that normal callousing does not take place, and this is an open invitation to some burrowing insects to complete the demise.

Some cultivars do seem to be more susceptible to rot than others. Usually the softer-type crowns succumb whereas the harder types seldom do. It should also be remembered that the environment which we provide is far removed from the original habitat of the delphinium's ancestors, which survived in much harsher conditions. There may also be a case for blaming plant breeders in the past who have, perhaps unwittingly, used susceptible plants as part of their breeding programme. It follows that it would be unwise to use such plants in any hybridisation scheme.

This malady should be put in perspective. With sensible cultivation it rarely occurs and many enthusiasts have never experienced rot during years of concentrated planting.

VIRUS

My reference books seem to state that the only virus which attacks delphiniums is the 'cucumber mosaic virus'. I am prepared to accept this, but it must be said that there have been no published scientific investigations on virus in delphiniums for the past fifty years; this is no doubt due to the fact that it is not regarded as a serious problem.

Some leading authorities believe that it is only seed-borne, while the fact that it is recessive suggests that it may be soil-borne. Whatever the cause, it is probably prudent to destroy any affected plants and, when propagating, a sterilised blade should be used to prevent the spread of the virus.

An affected plant is easy to spot. The first signs are a narrowing of the leaves with a distinct pointed appearance; this is sometimes coupled with yellowish streaks or veining. Soon the affected part will become stunted. Curiously enough, this yellowish marbling can occur in some cultivars such as 'Hilda Lucas', and may well be a form of virus, yet in these cases the vigour of the plant is not affected at all. I well remember the first batch of cuttings taken by the raiser of 'Hilda Lucas' over thirty years ago. Most of them exhibited this yellow streaking the following year and yet the plants have flourished. Successive generations of plants from cuttings still produce this mottling without any deterioration. It is also well established that virus is responsible for some yellowing of leaf structure in other plants, including trees

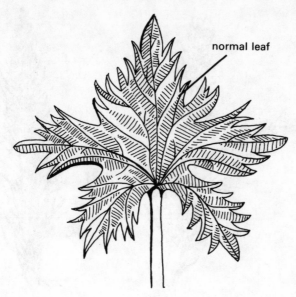

normal leaf

Normal delphinium leaf.

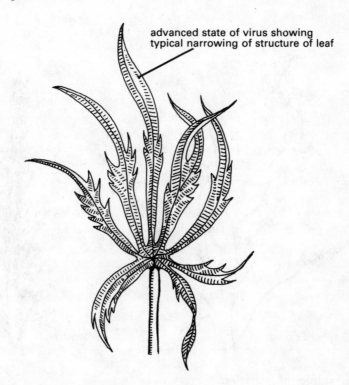

advanced state of virus showing
typical narrowing of structure of leaf

The effect of virus on the delphinium plant.

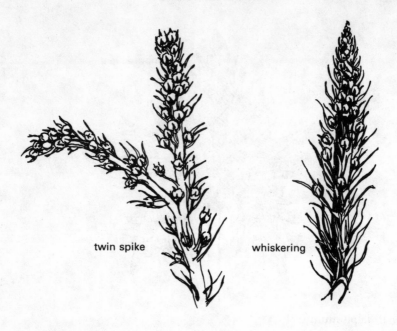

twin spike   whiskering

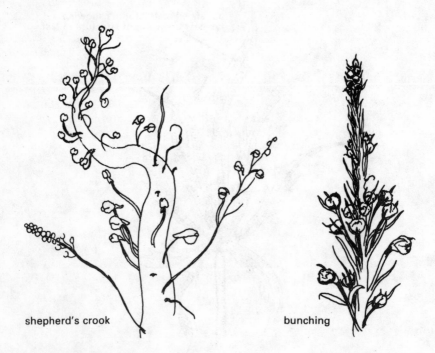

shepherd's crook   bunching

Examples of fasciation.

Blue Nile

Charles Gregory Broan

Moonbeam

Cream Cracker

Blackmore & Langdon's, near Bristol

Ruby   Layla

Gillian Dallas

Lord Butler

Our Deb

Giotto

Masquerade   Aphrodite

Dora Larkan   Crown Jewel

Spindrift

University Hybrid

Snowdon

Vespers

Tiddles   Strawberry Fair

Fanfare   Cherub

RHS Gardens at Wisley, Surrey

Leonora   Emily Hawkins

Chelsea Star   Joan Edwards

Butterball

Clack's Choice

Bruce

Claire

Min

Blue Nile

Royal Flush

Sandpiper

Faust

University Hybrid   Fenella

University Hybrid

Olive Poppleton

Clacks Farm, Worcester

Kathleen Cooke

Conspicuous

Skyline

Alice Artindale

Mighty Atom

Conspicuous

Gillian Dallas

Loch Leven

Wheatear

Thelma Rowe

Nimrod

Rosemary Brock

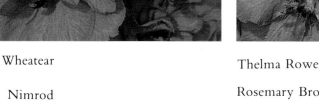

Chelsea Star

Mighty Atom

Silver Jubilee

Gordon Forsyth

and shrubs, which do not suffer any loss of vigour. The problem was highlighted a few years ago in the trials at Wisley when a delphinium, thought to be suffering with virus, was examined by the pathology department, who pronounced that the plant in question was suffering from a physiological disorder and not virus; and yet the symptoms were similar.

FASCIATION

This malformation is not a disease, but is regarded as a physiological disorder. Many other plants are affected from time to time. In the case of the delphinium the abnormality takes the form of a distorted and flattened flower spike and, at times, the shoot may divide into separate flower spikes. Less extreme examples are referred to as 'whiskering'. In these cases there is a complete absence of laterals, and in their place masses of whisker-like growths appear on the stem below the florets.

Unscientific theories abound as to the cause of this malfunction. Some suggest that it is a form of plant 'indigestion', when a massive intake of plant food occurs after a period of slow growth due to inclement growing conditions. Others claim that heavy frosts can contribute to the damage. Many botanists feel that insect damage during the formation of the embryo spike is the cause. Whatever the reason, it is a comparatively rare occurrence, although it does seem that some cultivars are more prone to this disorder than others which are seldom attacked.

7

Introducing a New Delphinium

THE ROYAL HORTICULTURAL SOCIETY

It is not generally appreciated, even by some horticultural tradesmen who sell delphiniums at nurseries or garden centres, that the Royal Horticultural Society is the international body authorised solely by the International Horticultural Congress to maintain a register of named delphiniums and to conduct trials of new cultivars. Reputable raisers throughout the world are aware of this, and those delphiniums which are not registered and/or which have not been awarded a certificate by the Royal Horticultural Society can nearly always be regarded with justifiable scepticism.

Registration

This is a simple process. You write off for a form to the Royal Horticultural Society (*see* page 138 for address), fill it in, giving a description of the delphinium as well as the name you have chosen, and return it with the appropriate modest fee. Of course, a name already registered cannot be used again, and it is as well to provide alternatives as many popular or obvious names have already been used by raisers over the past sixty years. In due course the Royal Horticultural Society will send to you a handsome certificate to prove registration, and this represents a guarantee that your chosen name cannot be repeated.

SUBMITTING A SEEDLING FOR TRIAL

The delphinium has always played a significant part in the various trials at the Royal Horticultural Society's grounds at

74

Wisley in Surrey. A committee is elected each year consist-
ing of representatives from the Royal Horticultural Society
and the Delphinium Society, and the trial of some 250 plants
is under the control of a trials officer who is a permanent
employee of the Royal Horticultural Society. These trials are
of considerable importance and attract visitors from all over
the world, serving as a 'shop window' for the critical
examination of new cultivars.

However, it is not easy to have a new seedling accepted for
trial. As with registration, a form should be obtained either
from the Delphinium Society or the Royal Horticultural
Society. This, when completed, should be submitted with
three cut spikes to the joint committee in London. This pre-
judging is carried out to ensure that only promising seedlings
are seen growing at the trial grounds. There are three
categories:

1. Cultivars suitable as show flowers.
2. Cultivars suitable as cut flowers.
3. Cultivars suitable for ordinary garden purposes.

A seedling may be entered under one or all of these categories, but a preliminary award may only be given in the
case of a show flower. In the other two cases awards will
only be given after trial.

THE WISLEY TRIALS

Three plants of the seedling recommended by the joint
committee must be supplied to the trials officer at Wisley,
where they are planted alongside all the other delphiniums
already selected. All plants receive similar treatment so that
objective comparisons can be made. The year following the
planting will be the first time when the entry will be judged
by the joint committee, which visits the trials on at least two
occasions when all the plants are given critical examination.
It is even possible that the raiser may be fortunate enough to
receive an award in the first year, but this is a very rare event,
for the awards are not given lightly and a more likely result
will be a resolution that the entry should be examined again
the following year. It will not be necessary to submit further
plants as the propagation department at Wisley will produce
its own material from the original crowns.

If, however, a plant has performed badly and is considered to be inferior it could be rejected and withdrawn from the trial. However, let us suppose that it receives an award! Until 1992 there were three categories: the top award was the First Class Certificate (FCC), which was only given to out-standing seedlings, and was usually reserved for plants which were a distinct break in a new direction, whether in colour, form or character; the next award was an Award of Merit (AM); and lastly there was the award of Highly Commended (HC). Plants could remain in the trial for many years and year by year they could be considered to be sufficiently good enough to move up from an HC to an AM and finally to a FCC. In 1992 this award system was replaced with one award category only. Known as the Award of Garden Merit, it will only be given after the plant has performed satisfactorily for two years at the Wisley trials.

After an award is given the plant is examined in detail by the trials department and a full report is recorded in the register, so that anyone requiring the cultivar can obtain full information, including a reliable source. Initially, these details are recorded in the current edition of the Delphinium Society's year book, but from time to time the register is updated to show all plants which have received awards and copies are obtainable from the Royal Horticultural Society.

A typical entry might appear as follows:

'Blue Heaven' (raised by Mr Raiser; introduced by Supplier Nurseries) FCC 28th June, 1988. Plant 198.1 to 228.6cm tall. Flower spike 91.5 to 96.4cm, long, tapering. Florets closely spaced of 7.6cm diameter. Many side-shoots. Outer sepals a colour somewhat deeper than Blue Group 101C, flushed towards base with Violet Group 100C, heavily flushed and streaked with Violet Group 84C. Eye a slightly deeper blue than Blue Group 100C streaked with Violet Group 84C. Flowering from 20th June, 1984 (AM 1985).

The reference to colour, using a code system, is based on the Royal Horticultural Society's colour code book, copies of which are obtainable from them.

The relationship between the Delphinium Society and the Royal Horticultural Society is a co-operative, fruitful and happy one, and any newcomer wishing to have plants of his raising submitted for trial will find the officials of either society to be very friendly and helpful. If you have raised a real 'winner' which subsequently receives an award, you can justifiably feel quite proud, and the pleasure of knowing that your efforts have been recognised by two such important institutions and have received publicity is a fine reward. This satisfaction can even be surpassed when you are visiting one of the shows of the Delphinium Society, and you observe a spike of a plant raised by you receiving a top prize on the show bench, having been entered by a complete stranger.

(One word of warning: be careful in your choice of name. To use the name of a loved one requires great caution, for the first expectations of a seedling may not be fulfilled in subsequent years, and the cultivar may have degenerative qualities to the point where it may not be worth growing. Once you have used and registered the name of, for example, your spouse, it will not be possible to use it again. For obvious reasons, this can cause much heartache.)

8
Delphiniums for Exhibition

Much of the theory concerning cultivation for garden purposes applies equally as well to the delphinium grown for exhibition purposes. It must be emphasised, however, that in order to produce the giant spikes of between 3 to 5ft (90–150cm) of actual bloom, some additional attention must be given to the plants.

Many growers consider that too much emphasis has been placed on size, and some enthusiasts consider that such large spikes are out of character and, perhaps, appear coarse. Whilst one must have some sympathy with this view, a well-grown large spike can be a magnificent sight, and some cultivars are able to stand an increase in size without any loss of that ethereal quality that is so typical of the genus.

Of the utmost importance is the selection of cultivars. Some beautiful delphiniums will never produce a spike capable of competing on the show bench. There is, however, a wide choice, covering all colours as well as the period of actual blooming. This latter point is particularly important, and a selection of early, mid–season and late blooming cultivars is vital for timing a specific show date. Make a selection from those types that are successful entries at shows, especially those held at the Royal Horticultural Society's halls at Westminster, and at Wisley. All of the following have performed well over past years in London:

'Mighty Atom'	'Spindrift'
'Blue Nile'	'Loch Nevis'
'Emily Hawkins'	'Gossamer'
'Fanfare'	'Loch Lomond'
'Gordon Forsythe'	'Summer Wine'
'Joyce Roffey'	'Loch Leven'
'Kathleen Cooke'	'Sungleam'
'Bruce'	'Chelsea Star'
'Sandpiper'	'Gillian Dallas'

'Royal Flush'   'Summerfield Miranda'
'Fenella'   'Rosemary Brock'
'Olive Poppleton'   (*see* Chapter 12)

CULTURAL REQUIREMENTS

To obtain the larger-sized spike rather more space is required between plants than between those grown for garden decoration. A distance of 30in (75cm) each way will not only ensure that there is no competition for nutrients, but will also give the grower the room to attend to each plant without fear of damage to neighbouring plants. An open site is required and at all costs you should avoid planting near to competing roots of trees, hedges and shrubs. With these taller, pampered, exhibition plants it is a mistake to position them in a place where a 'wind tunnel' effect can occur. This can often happen between buildings, and a stream of turbulent air can build up for a considerable distance beyond the actual buildings – this can have a devastating effect on spikes heavy with water from a summer storm.

Thinning

One of the most important contributions that can be made is to ensure that adequate thinning is carried out at an early stage. A well-grown, one-year-old plant is incapable of producing more than two exhibition spikes, and even an established plant should never be allowed to carry more than five.

Feeding

However thoroughly the ground may have been prepared with generous additions of organic matter, some extra nutrients will be required. Nitrogen can often be in short supply, especially after a wet period when this nutrient can be leached away from the feeding roots. So a dressing of a fertiliser rich in nitrogen should be given in early spring, when the shoots are 3–4in (7.5–10cm) high. Not wishing to enter into the controversial realm of 'organic versus non-organic' materials, I will just say that either type will produce the end result needed. Apart from, possibly, dried blood, inorganic fertilisers tend to act more quickly, and to that extent they have an advantage even if long-term effects may be harmful to the soil structure. Whatever you choose, they all have one thing in common and that is rate of application. Always obey the recommended instructions shown on the packaging. Giving a 'bit extra for luck' is wasteful, and indeed may be harmful. Potash applied some six weeks before the spike is mature will help considerably in hardening the tissues and will act as an insurance against fracture.

Staking

Of the two methods in Chapter 5, my own preference is for one cane per shoot with a firm anchor tie at about 12in (30cm) from ground level. This will often be enough, but in extremely windy sites a further loose tie some 6in (15cm) below the bottom floret may be advisable, allowing the spike to sway in windy weather but to remain firm against the cane adjacent to the anchor tie. Because heights vary it may be necesary to remove part of the cane with secateurs if it protrudes into the florets.

Watering

This factor is most important. If soil preparation has been thorough, and if a mulch of organic matter has been used early on, then watering becomes less necessary. However, delphiniums bloom in Britain in the warmest part of the year, and drought conditions can prevail at this time. However good your feeding programme may have been, this will be to little avail if there is a shortage of moisture in the soil. Clearly, the type of soil that you have matters. Well-drained, sandy soils will almost certainly require additional supplies of water, whereas other types will tend to retain moisture rather better.

Hard as it may be to believe, there is seldom enough rainfall in most parts of Britain to satisfy the requirements of potential exhibition plants. If you are in any doubt, then you must water. Indeed, it is almost impossible to overwater delphiniums during their growing period when they can put on as much as 3in (7.5cm) of growth in one day during June. One difficulty in giving advice on the amount of water to provide is due to the fact that mains pressure varies enormously, but what can be said without fear of contradiction is that a mere sprinkling is no good at all. A thorough soaking must be given, and this means, in most areas, leaving the spinkler in position from between half an hour and three hours, depending on pressure. A simple way of ensuring that enough is being given is to place a bucket under the main area of spray, and to stop watering only when this is filled with a few inches of water.

There are really no secret potions or formulas for success. It is simply a matter of treating your delphiniums as you would attend to the cultural requirements of a successful vegetable garden, where fertile soil, thinning, feeding and watering lead to bumper crops.

SHOWING

There are a number of practices which exhibitors of other flowers use in order to ensure that their blooms are in the best possible condition when the judging takes place. Rose growers tie blooms together with soft wool and use refrigerators to keep them cool. Gladioli fanciers use dark cupboards and variations in artificial temperatures. Exercises such as these are not used with the delphinium, and this is no doubt due to their size and the fact that the average show spike will have upwards of fifty opened florets. Happily, there is no need to have recourse to these doubtful practices, for a spike will remain in show condition for several days, and even longer if conditions are cool.

Entry Forms and Selection

Most local societies and the Delphinium Society require submission of entry forms at least one week before the date of the show. Beginners find it difficult to select those blooms which will be at the right stage so far in advance. There are, however, a number of guidelines which can help and which will enable you to complete the entry form with reasonable confidence. In average weather conditions you can expect a period of about three weeks to elapse from the time the embryo spike is seen until maturity. In addition, a spike will usually be at its best one week after the bottom florets have just opened and it will take a further five days for the majority of the florets to be fully developed.

It is quite normal to show a spike which is not fully

opened and in fact most prize-winners selected are perhaps only three-quarters open, for judges are looking for a spike which is in fresh condition rather than one which has become 'tired'. The Delphinium Society has recommened that a spike should be as fully opened as possible, but not at the expense of dropping florets: stripped stems and florets showing seed pods will be deemed serious faults.

Appearance

The overall appearance of the staged spike will have a considerable influence on the judges. The florets should be evenly distributed so that the final effect is one of a well-furnished bloom, but at the same time the flower should not be overcrowded with florets overlapping one another. Length of spike is of importance but never when it spoils the character of the particular cultivar. Pyramidal-shaped spikes usually find more favour than thin columnar cultivars, and a spike which is bent and not perfectly straight will be regarded as a fault.

Florets

The requirements of individual florets are less easy to define. They should of course be fully open, except the topmost ones (as already mentioned), and they should be of uniform character throughout. The sepals should be firm and of good substance with consistent regular eyes. Judges will often reject spikes where the florets are cupped in shape, or where they hang downwards, or, alternatively, face upwards. Avoid any seedlings of your own raising which have thin petals. Those which have a 'waxy' look are the ones to choose.

There is no doubt about it that judges are only human and tend to be influenced by spikes which have well-defined contrasting eyes. Any spikes where the eyes are untidy or ragged-looking, and especially where the colours have spilled over into the adjacent petals, as sometimes happens even with outstanding cultivars, will be passed by.

Colour

At the larger shows, and particularly at the Delphinium Society's shows, classes exist calling for separate colours.

This can cause difficulties, particularly with seedlings which have not been registered and, therefore, have not been described in any reference book. For example, a specific class may call for only blue spikes. To be absolutely accurate, there has never been a delphinium which is entirely blue, even though a casual examination may give the impression of the colour, and a closer inspection will reveal other veins of colour in the petals, ranging from pink shades to purple segments. Fortunately, both the judges and the show secretary are aware of this factor and, providing the general appearance is blue, all will be well. There are also classes for pink shades, when really no elatum-type delphinium exists which is a true pink − it is the so-called dusky-pink delphiniums which are entered in these sections. Perhaps most debatable of all are the white classes where, apart from petal shade, the colour of the eye can range from white to black, with other colours, including browns and honey, in between. The colour of the eye is discounted and, providing the overall appearance is near-white or off-white, the bloom will not be marked 'NAS' (not according to schedule).

If you are in any doubt it is a good idea to discuss a doubtful entry with the show secretary whose decision in the Delphinium Society is final and can override that of the judges. Finally, a situation can occur when the judges cannot easily make up their minds on a particular class where two spikes appear to be of equal merit. The one which has the cleanest colour will generally be favoured.

Laterals

Because of the difficulty of transporting delphiniums to shows, a long-held rule that spikes should be shown with a minimum of three laterals was dropped some years ago by the Delphinium Society. Today, no differentiation is made between those entries shown with laterals and those shown without. There are, however, separate classes for laterals, and generally speaking the same values apply to these most useful appendages as to the main spikes.

Classes for Individual Florets

Becoming increasingly popular at the Delphinium Society's shows are the classes for florets. The national shows always call for six florets per entry, and the matter of paramount

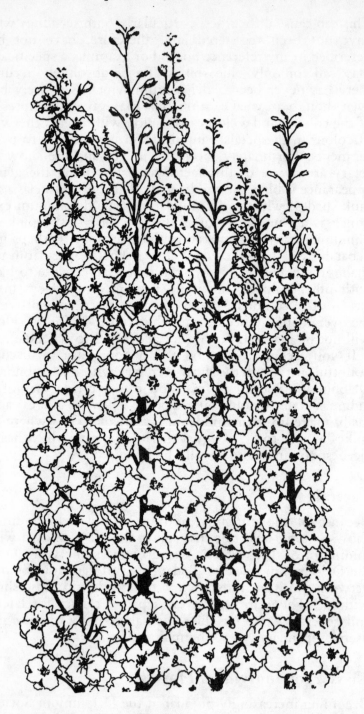

An established plant. Note that all trace of the supporting
stakes is hidden.

importance is the matching quality of blooms. All six should be uniform and the winner will almost certainly come from an entry where the florets are like the proverbial 'peas in a pod'. A final decision on closely similar entries will often be made on the neat way in which they are presented, so it always pays to spend some time over the arranging.

PREPARATION BEFORE THE SHOW

It is far better to cut the spike from the plant with a sharp knife rather than to use secateurs which tend to crush the stem. The most crucial decision, concerning the timing of the cutting, depends on the weather. Unfortunately, weather forecasts cannot always be relied upon, and very often you will need to 'guesstimate' the chances of rain in your own particular locality. If you are in any doubt, my advice is to cut all the spikes required the evening before the show. Nothing is more hopeless than attempting to transport wet spikes to a show, for by the time you and they arrive they will only be fit for the compost heap.

Having cut the spikes with an oblique cut, the best thing to do is to fill them with water. This is, admittedly, a tricky operation, but it does much to preserve freshness. Take a small watering-can, of the type used for indoor pot plants, hold the spike at an angle of around 45°, and let the water trickle into the hollow stem. Some exhibitors plug the end with cotton wool, but I favour placing the thumb over the end and then gently lowering the spike, with the thumb firmly in place, into a water-filled container.

Recently there have been some developments in the cut flower trade using chemicals to help preserve blooms for quite lengthy periods. The best are based on silver nitrate and there is no doubt that steeping the cut blooms in the correct solution of one of these flower preservatives can achieve astonishing results, keeping them in pristine condition for a considerable time. Unfortunately, these superior cut flower preservatives are not commercially available yet, and to obtain a supply you may have to beg for some from a professional horticulturalist. They should not be confused with preparations already freely available which, in my opinion, do little to help the preservation of large flowers such as exhibition delphiniums.

Having placed your blooms into vessels containing water (with or without preservatives), you place them under cover to avoid rain, or a heavy condensation of dew. It is even possible that you may have been forced to cut them after rain, in which case a room with a modest amount of warmth will dry them out overnight. It is best, however, to store them in a cool place, such as a shed, garage or outhouse. This will not apply if it is possible under the rules to stage the day before the show. This is always to be preferred, for it gives the transported spikes enough time to recover from packing. It never ceases to amaze me that even a badly-crushed spike will recover to a normal configuration when it has been staged overnight.

Travelling

It may not be possible for many reasons to stage until the morning of the show and then even more careful packing is required for the journey from your home to the show ground. The professional will transport the spikes in containers of water in a van with at least 6ft (180cm) of headroom. Apart from sedate driving, no other care is needed, and no problems are likely to occur if you are fortunate enough to have such a facility available. However, most amateurs have to carry them flat. Most have the use of a motor car and clearly the estate or hatchback type is the best vehicle to use – the front passenger seat may have to be removed if your only choice is a saloon car. At the last possible moment, pack the blooms into layers separated by masses of tissue paper – the more tissue used the better, as it has a wonderful cushioning effect if lightly crushed. Some exhibitors will pack the spikes filled with water and plugged with cotton wool, whilst others will carry the blooms 'dry' on the grounds that the extra weight of water tends to crush the florets more easily.

For those who do not have the facility of a car, all is not lost. A friendly electrical shop may give you the boxes used to house fluorescent light tubes. These are about 6ft (180cm) in length and will accommodate four spikes comfortably, as long as you wrap each one in tissue paper. The boxes are then easy to transport with you.

Staging

On arrival at the show your first priority, even before you chat to all your friends and acquaintances, is to unpack your spikes and place them in the water-filled vases provided. Do not bother about order – the most important task is to get them in an upright position as soon as possible. Then at your leisure you can sort the spikes out into the various classes which you have entered, and spend more time in preparing them for the vase. The aim must be to keep the spikes as fresh as possible. There are three methods used by the seasoned exhibitor, and there is no evidence to prove that one is better than another – I suspect that in the end they all achieve the desired effect. You must form your own opinion and adopt whichever course you prefer. All do have one common factor and that is the making of a fresh oblique cut to the stem with a sharp knife, so that if the cut end rests on the bottom of the vase there will still be a space for the water to enter the stem.

The most popular procedure, having made this fresh slanting cut, is to fill the stem with water, taking care to let it trickle in slowly in order to prevent an air-lock. This requires a certain knack and, above all, confidence. With the thumb firmly in place, return the spike to an upright position and lower the spike into the vase with the thumb still in position under the water. Release the thumb and gently lower the spike into the full depth of the vase. The theory is that capillary action will continue to draw the water up the stem, since there is no air present to prevent the flow.

The second method is somewhat similar, much favoured by flower arrangers, and is known as 'conditioning'. The only difference is that a plug of cotton wool takes the place of the thumb, and is kept in place. The theory is that water continues to flow through the permeable cotton wool.

The final way, and the easiest of all, is to place the spike, without any water in the stem, in the vase and then to make the slanting cut *under water* with secateurs. Those who favour this method argue that water is drawn up – not in the hollow stem, but in the plant tissues present in the wall of the spike. The cutting under water is said to prevent an air-lock.

Whatever method you adopt, take just one spike at a time for it is usual for spikes to be presented singly in each vase. Make certain that the cut is made in the right place, to ensure that when the bloom is in the vase the spike conforms with the standard of uniformity set by the Delphinium Society. A flower spike, of say, 2ft (60cm) in length would not present a satisfactory appearance if 8in (20cm) or more of stem were visible above the rim of the vase, whereas a spike of twice the length would look presentable with a longer visible stem. Always try to make the cut so that the amount of visible stem between the bottom florets and the top of the vase is in proportion to the overall length of the flower portion.

In order to keep the spike upright in the vase some exhibitors use paper as a packing around the stem. This is not very satisfactory as it can soon become soggy and, after an hour or so, the spike can lean out of the perpendicular, presenting the distinct danger of the whole vase falling over. A far better method is to use slices of the discarded stem as packing. Finally, use a few delphinium leaves around the stem – this will improve the appearance even if it will not affect the judging.

Always have a final look around, for sometimes it may be prudent to swap spikes from one class to another, with the object of strengthening one class at the expense of others where it seems obvious there is no chance of an award.

Above all, treat it as fun and as a contribution to making the show a success. In some years you may not receive a single award, whereas in others you may 'sweep the board'. If you have never competed in a flower show before do try it, for as a novice you will receive friendly assistance from most seasoned exhibitors, and to attempt an entry is the best possible way of learning the art.

9
Delphiniums for Decoration

FLOWER ARRANGEMENT

Delphiniums are much in demand for floral art. Why should this be so? Firstly, the main spikes, which can measure anything from 18in to 4ft (45–120cm) of actual bloom, are almost indispensable for massed arrangements planned on the grand scale. Secondly, with careful planning, they can be available from early summer right through the year until the first frosts, and laterals are so useful for the more dainty arrangements. Thirdly, and never to be overlooked, individual florets can measure from 2–3in (5–7.5cm) across and come provided with long pedicels which are often as much as 12in (30cm) in length. Finally, the genus will dry very satisfactorily.

The Large Arrangement

There are few places in the modern small house where exhibition blooms could be used to effect, although you should not immediately dismiss a hall or even a fireplace. It is, however, in the foyer of a hospital, or the reception areas of hotels, institutions, clubs and businesses, where these large arrangements are indispensable. They are also most useful in church, on pedestals, where lofty arrangements are needed so that they are visible to the congregation.

You should not refrain from using large spikes from the garden where the bottom florets are past their best. Simply remove all the faded and dropping florets so that one is left with a flower length more akin to the size of a lateral. When these spikes are removed carefully from the plant, it is possible to leave intact the laterals which are in evidence, although by no means mature.

Laterals

Most well-grown delphiniums will produce side-shoots, known more correctly as laterals. On an average plant there will be from three to six and, as these range in overall length from 12–30in (30–75cm), they are ideal for the more modest-sized arrangements suitable for the home.

Never overlook the semi-immature lateral. These can be useful in providing the blue of the florets which are open and the blue/green of the unopened buds. Used with foliage from other plants they can create a most pleasing, cool effect at a time when we experience our warmest weather. They are particularly welcome in compositions requiring horizontal blooms for, unlike many other spiky flowers, there is no tendency to curl upwards, as is often the case with flowers of, say, the lupin family.

Florets

Delphinium florets are absolutely ideal for the dining table. When you consider that a spike will produce anything from forty to eighty florets over a period of about three weeks, you can readily appreciate why they are in much demand by floral art societies. They are also very popular with professional florists who use them to great effect in delightful bouquets and head-dresses especially for June and July weddings – the white florets are especially superb for a bride's bouquet.

For the table the blue tones are an ideal foil for the dainty blooms of, for example, escallonia, whereas the dusky-pink tones blend extremely well with pinks such as 'Doris' which, like escallonia, bloom at the same time as delphiniums.

Drying

Selection is of the utmost importance if you are to be successful. Fully mature spikes will shed their florets, but if you are prepared to spend some time with the fully-developed spike it can be very useful. If the florets are carefully removed, laid head downwards on newspaper, and placed in an airing cupboard or sunless place to dry, they can be mounted on wires after drying has been completed. These can be most useful in the depths of winter in conjunction with evergreen foliage.

The usual course is to choose only half-opened spikes or laterals and to hang these upside down in a cool place to dry. Laterals, due to their lower moisture content, dry exceptionally well.

CONTAINER-GROWN DELPHINIUMS

In spite of their comparative bulk, delphiniums grow remarkably well in the restricted environment of a pot. Proof of this statement may be seen every year at the Chelsea Flower Show, superb delphiniums are exhibited, all of which are grown in pots no larger than 10in (25cm). It is easy to establish the reason why delphiniums flourish when grown in a restricted manner, where other perennial subjects fail to produce satisfactory results. The feeding roots are all contained in the top 12in (30cm) of soil, so the delphinium is an almost ideal subject for pot culture.

If you are to have success it is vital to obtain young rooted cuttings from specialist growers, which are usually available from May to June in 3–4in (7.5–10cm) containers. Field-grown plants of larger size will never be satisfactory. The young cutting should be potted on to a 5in (12.5 cm) size using, preferably, a compost based on the John Innes formula. If, however, the only available growing medium is one of the many commercial peat-based potting composts, you must be prepared to 'doctor' the ingredients. In order to provide a really free-draining material, you should add at least one-third coarse sand to most proprietary brands, and to every 10in (25cm) pot an addition of 1oz (3g) of hydrated lime is needed to help flocuation. Firm potting is an essential requirement, paying particular attention to the compost around the edge of the pot, and modern plastic pots will be satisfactory – indeed, they are probably superior to the older clay types for watering will be needed less frequently.

An eye should be kept on these young plants to ensure that they do not dry out, and all flower spikes should be pinched out as soon as they are observed – however, you should never remove any of the leaf structure. After a very few weeks the pot will be full of roots and before the plant becomes pot-bound it should be moved on to a 7in (18cm) pot, using the same compost recommended earlier. Towards

91

the end of summer these young plants will be ready for their final pots, the 10in (25cm) size being ideal, although some really superb spikes can be obtained in 9in (23cm) sizes. They will require rather more attention as regards the frequency of watering. It is unnecessary to use any crocks in the base of the pots as often advocated in older publications, for the free-draining compost advised will be adequate. It is a good plan to stand the pots on a raised surface or, better still, on a free-draining surface made up of stones or coarse aggregate, in order to prevent worms from entering the pots through the drainage holes. These can severely curtail the vigorous development needed.

Throughout the growing period all flower spikes should be removed and towards the beginning of the autumn it will be necessary to add a feed, for the initial fertiliser will have become exhausted. To this end you should aim at producing fat embryo buds which form below the surface. A tomato-type fertiliser is perfect for this purpose, for it contains a high ratio of the potash that is so essential for the plant as dormancy nears with approaching winter. It is better to choose one of the more modern types which are freely available in a completely soluble form rather than the granular, for the food will be available immediately and can conveniently be added when watering.

The actual siting of the pots is not critical, but do try to avoid extremes of sunshine or shade. The ideal would be an aspect which receives some shade from the midday sun for this will help cut down the frequency of watering.

With the approach of winter the top growth will start to die down and by the end of November all vegetation may be removed and the pots generally tidied up. During the winter months the pots can be placed in any position for they will survive the extremes of temperature found in Britain and they will then require no further attention since winter rains will provide all the moisture needed.

EARLY BLOOMING

It is a simple matter to have delphiniums in bloom at least one month earlier than normal if you enjoy the facility of a moderately heated glass structure, and even plants in an unheated one will produce earlier spikes than the open ground. It is also surprising how much earlier than normal you can produce flowers by standing the pots against the south wall of a house. The sheltered environment of the wall also raises the surrounding temperature due to the thermal efficiency of brickwork.

It is a mistake to move those plants intended for glass-house culture inside before the middle of January. A period of complete dormancy is required in order to prevent premature growth which would only lead to undersized spikes.

If there is one secret of success with pot culture it is ensuring that there is an adequate supply of plant food available before summer recommences. The winter rains will have leached out most of the plant food, especially nitrogen, and so an application of a complete feed should be given, choosing a soluble fertiliser with a high nitrogen formula, as soon as the plants are housed. The instructions on the package should be followed closely and you should avoid the temptation to add a little extra for it can lead to abnormally tall and therefore unmanageable growth.

TREATMENT DURING THE GROWING PERIOD

Those plants which will remain outside will require a similar feed to those under cover, but in these cases the application is best delayed until late January. Thereafter treatment is the same wherever the pots are sited.

As with plants in the open garden, the shoots of the pot-grown plants will show signs of growth early on in the new year. Some cultivars will produce an abundance of shoots and because of the restrictive nature of the pot, the thinning must be more drastic than with those in the open ground. On most cultivars one shoot only should be retained, choosing the most vigorous. There are some named plants which are exceptionally strong-growing and it is possible to allow as many as three shoots to mature. It will be quite obvious to determine the number which may be left, and as a guide those shoots smaller than the thickness of a pencil should be removed.

As growth extends, watering must never be overlooked, for the pots will now be completely filled with roots, and allowing the compost to dry out would only lead to dis-appointment. Feeding will also be required, perhaps with each watering – again, follow the instructions. Some products call for weaker applications with constant watering, whilst others recommend an addition of fertilisers with every other watering.

Staking is a simple matter for the sides of the pots add security to the stakes and quite short canes are all that are needed.

The plants being grown under protection can be brought out into the open at any time. If this process is carried out over a period of several weeks you can have delphiniums in flower from early May, to adorn your terrace or patio, followed by those growing against a south wall, and, finally, by those grown in an ordinary position, resulting in a colourful and unusual display right through until the end of July.

TREATMENT AFTER FLOWERING

A delphinium in a pot after flowering can be a very sorry sight. Luckily, it is an easy matter to remove the offending object to a less conspicuous place. You can let it remain in its position for another year or, alternatively, cut it down completely to the top of the pot and feed and water generously so that it can be an adornment with a second blooming in the late summer or early autumn. There is a further alternative which is practised by some growers. These delphiniums make excellent stock plants for propagation and may be left in the pots until the following spring, when they will provide a considerable number of cuttings. They may also be planted out in the garden for the same purpose, but do not expect them to produce blooms as well as those grown naturally in the open ground.

10

A Delphinium Calendar

I have noticed in other books on horticultural matters that when a calendar has been produced, more often than not, the phrase 'tasks for the month' appears. I have avoided this because, to me, the very word 'task' indicates some endeavour which is not pleasurable. I have found most of the activities needed to grow delphiniums to be, on the whole, rather enjoyable, and I hope that you too will be able to have fun when attending to the cultural needs of this beautiful flower. I have also placed an emphasis on the real possibility of having delphiniums in bloom from May, right up until the first frost, when they are grown outside. With the assistance of a moderately heated glasshouse the season can quite easily be extended until Christmas.

Of course, much that will be covered in the calendar has already been mentioned in greater detail elsewhere, and readers should refer to the main narrative for explication when it is needed.

JANUARY

Under Glass

Those who have a moderately-heated greenhouse, with just enough to keep the frost out, can really get a head start. If the house is also sited in a position to receive maximum light and sunshine it is astonishing what can be accomplished with the delphinium.

To germinate satisfactorily, the seeds of a delphinium require cool conditions, and even in the depths of winter the pot or seed tray should be sited in a position where the rays of the sun will never touch it. An ideal place is under a shelf – this way, you can keep an eye on progress, and at the same time the gentle warmth will be enough to enable germination

95

to take place in about four weeks, after which the container should be moved to a lighter position, perhaps on top of the shelf.

This month is ideal for the housing of stools, or stock plants in pots, for the purposes of taking cuttings. In the former case, having lifted the plant from the open ground around the middle of January, all soil should be removed. This is most easily accomplished by using the force of water from the jet of a hose. As long as you are careful not to use too high a pressure, you will end up with a perfectly clean crown and a mass of fibrous roots completely undamaged – this may not be the case if you try to remove the soil with a tool. The clean stool should then be boxed up with peat in a standard depth seed tray, so that the actual crown is proud of the surface, and only the fibrous roots are covered. If a sunny spell follows the housing of the stools or pots, then it is incredible how quickly shoots will appear of sufficient length for propagation. Up to 2 or 3in (5–7.5cm) of growth can easily take place in a matter of ten days or so, which is the ideal length for severing the growths close to the crown.

In the congenial atmosphere of a greenhouse you will soon appreciate the advantages over securing cuttings from a plant in the open ground. Not only is your own comfort assured, but the wisdom of placing the stool in peat so that the crown is proud will also become apparent. It will be easy to see exactly where the new shoot joins the plant, and this is where the cut *must* be made. The actual rooting can take place in the glasshouse, using one of the methods advocated earlier. The water cutting method, or a variation on it, has advantages, because you can add further cuttings to the same receptacle as and when they become available over the following weeks.

Outside

It is accepted by all delphinium enthusiasts that slugs and delphiniums cohabit, and the former must be destroyed if you are to have vigorous plants. If you have any doubts concerning the measures you have already taken for control, it is essential to tackle the problem again now. You cannot do better for protection than using a solution of 2oz aluminium sulphate to 1 gallon of water applied to approximately 4 sq yds (about 6g/9litres for 4 sq m) concentrating the liquid around the crown. This strong solution is safe at this time of year, for any toxic effects will have dispersed before growth commences. Follow this treatment with methiocarb-based pellets, at the rates recommended, and you can be confident that, for the time being, you will have slug-free delphiniums.

FEBRUARY

Under Glass

Autumn-sown seedlings which have been overwintered outside will benefit from being given some form of glass protection in the early part of this month. A frame sited in a sunny position will suffice, but a heated glasshouse will produce earlier growth. Do not worry if the dormant seedlings in their seed trays are covered with snow or are frozen solid. Simply shake the snow off and place the tray under glass where regrowth will soon take place. By the end of the month they will have developed sufficiently for a transfer into 4in (10cm) pots.

Seed sown in early January will be sufficiently advanced to be pricked out 2in (5cm) apart each way into a standard-sized seed tray.

Cuttings should be examined frequently and you will readily appreciate the water cutting methods, for you will be able to see at a glance if rooting has taken place. Any which have produced roots, however small, should be potted up into 3in (7.5cm) containers and left in a shady place for a week or two.

Continue to take cuttings as and when they become available. It is a good plan to water the stools used for propagation with a weak solution of a soluble plant fertiliser.

Plants growing in pots for the patio should be thinned, leaving only the strongest shoots. Follow this operation with a liquid feed which has a high nitrogen factor, in order to build up vigorous growth.

Outside

Because the delphinium is one of the earliest of all hardy perennial plants to appear, growth will almost certainly be apparent above the soil in the south during the early part of the month, although this will be a week or two later in the north. If anti-slug precautions have not been taken, it is possible that some damage may have been caused and so it is vital to wage war on these pests now. Use only 1oz of aluminium sulphate to the gallon (3g/9 litres) at this time of the year, as a stronger solution could cause damage to the growing tissues. Follow this operation with a dressing of methiocarb-based pellets.

One unpleasant thing remains for those who wish to increase their favourite delphiniums and who do not possess a glasshouse – and this *is* a 'task' – scrabbling for cuttings. I have taken many hundreds, perhaps thousands, this way, but I confess that it is an operation for the young or sprightly, and for those who are impervious to the cold. It really does mean getting down on all fours, and gently teasing the soil away from the crown of the plant until you expose that part where the potential cuttings join. Using a sharp knife you should take the required number, 2–3in (5–7.5cm) long, choosing those which are of about the thickness of a pencil and leaving those which are larger to grow on to provide the flowering spikes. All spindly growth can be removed at the same time. There is always the danger when using this method that you might leave wounds through which disease and/or pests can cause weakening of the plant. You cannot take better precautions against this than to use the old-fashioned remedy of dressing the cuts with a dusting of powdered charcoal and sulphur, coupled with a modern soil insecticide. If, during these operations, you spot tiny, almost transparent white, globe-like objects around the crown, then you have potential trouble, for they are the eggs of slugs and it will mean that you failed to use the solution of aluminium sulphate recommended. If you had done so, these eggs would have been dissolved by the stringent action of the chemical. Take offensive action *before* they hatch.

Even if you do not require exhibition-sized spikes, late February is a good time to give the plants a dressing of a general fertiliser at the rate recommended, whether organic or chemical-based. Apart from dried blood, the latter has the advantage over the former, because of the speed with which it releases the plant foods.

Before other gardening work takes an ever-increasing share of your time, it is a good plan to have ready a supply of clean pots and the canes which will be needed for staking. To avoid passing on disease and pests it is wise both to wash the pots and to steep the ends of the canes in disinfectant.

Prepare sites intended for the planting of both rooted

cuttings and seedlings, but, unless you garden on badly water-logged soil, do not cultivate the site deeply. The hoe is the best tool, or the pronged cultivator. Aim at a depth of no more than 1–2in (2.5–5cm) and incorporate a slow-release plant food at the same time. This is where organic materials score over chemicals. I feel that one cannot use a better material than coarse-ground hoof and horn meal at around 4oz to the square yard (about 12g to the square metre). This will release plant foods slowly over several years.

If you do not possess any form of glass protection, you can still raise delphiniums from seed successfully, but they will be later. Simply obtain a wooden box from your greengrocer, knock the bottom out and fasten a sheet of polythene on the top with drawing pins. Prepare a patch of soil in a shady part of the garden by adding some peat and sharp sand over an area similar in size to the box, and broadcast a packet of seed, covering with the merest trace of sharp sand. Place the covered box in position, and in about eight to ten weeks the box can be removed in advance of the time when the seedlings will be large enough to transplant elsewhere. Like glasshouse-raised plants, one seedling to a 3in (7.5cm) pot is the best method – this way, when the time comes for planting there will be a minimum of disturbance, and the young plants will grow away with scarcely a check.

MARCH

Under Glass

Cuttings will still become available, but by the end of the month the only growth which will come from the depleted stock plants will be too thin for desirable cuttings and the spent plant should be removed and burnt. It is not wise to compost such old material as there is always the risk of passing on disease.

Early in the month the seedlings from the autumn sowing will be ready for a brief period of hardening off. An ideal spot is against a south wall, where a couple of weeks will be sufficient prior to planting out.

The January-sown plants will be smaller, but by the end of the month these too will have filled their pots nicely with roots. If, for any reason, it is impossible to plant out these young seedlings by, say, the middle of April, then they should be potted up into a 5in (12.5cm) pot. If they are left to become root-bound they will take very much longer to establish themselves in the open ground.

Many of the cuttings will also have made substantial growth in the 3in (7.5cm) pots. A hardening-off period is also required before planting out and, again, the little plants should be potted on to larger pots if there is a danger of them becoming pot-bound.

Ensure that the plants in pots for the patio do not become dry and continue to add liquid feeds in accordance with the instructions. The plants should be given a position of maximum light in order to prevent unnatural height at flowering time, and during mild periods they will benefit from being taken outside. This is exactly what the professional growers do, in order to time the date of blooming to coincide with early major flower shows such as Chelsea.

Outside

The autumn-sown seedlings will be ready by the end of the month, after hardening off, for planting out. If you have not already prepared the site as recommended in February, then it is better to plant the seedlings without disturbing the soil and rely on a top dressing of fertiliser, gently hoed in after planting has been accomplished. If the soil is on the dry side, as can often happen after March winds, then it is essential to water each plant thoroughly.

In some gardening books, especially those written many years ago, the reader is told to 'keep the hoe going'. I cannot find fault with this recommendation, and this tool suits the cultivation of the delphinium exceptionally well. It is a mistake to cultivate the soil around delphinium plants any deeper than approximately 1in (2.5cm), as all feeding roots are in the top 10in (25cm) or so, including a mass situated just below the surface. The plant will be damaged if you disturb the soil any deeper. The Dutch hoe is ideal for the cultivation required – it will keep down weeds and it will mix fertiliser to a sufficient depth. If it does cut down the loss of moisture by reducing capillary action, as suggested by some writers, then this is to the good.

Continue to take cuttings from plants in the open ground. In late districts and in cold springs, material suitable for cuttings can become available well into March and sometimes into April as well.

Slugs

You must keep up anti-slug treatment, especially where young, newly-planted stock is involved. Care must be exercised when using the recommended dilution of aluminium sulphate to prevent the liquid splashing on the foliage. Its caustic nature will 'burn' any green growth and, although it may not kill the plant, it will severely retard development. Keep the solution to the area around the plant, and follow this treatment with more methiocarb-based pellets.

APRIL

Under Glass

By the end of the month all the spring-sown seedlings will be ready for hardening off.

The cuttings from crowns taken inside will virtually all have rooted and should, by the middle of the month, be potted up ready for hardening off. If there has been a delay due to other pressures which necessitated potting up into larger pots, as advocated in March, then there is one most important cultural step which should not be overlooked. In their 5in (12.5cm) pots the cuttings (or seedlings) will make rapid growth, and surprisingly soon the young plants will endeavour to flower. The days will have lengthened and, as small and as young as they are, they will naturally try to flower at the normal time, which is from June to July. You must prevent this from happening. The finger and thumb are most useful gardening implements, and you should use them to nip out the embryo flowering spike as soon as it is observed, but never the foliage. This action has the effect of transferring all the growing energy into the formation of the developing crown, and lays a good foundation for the long-term prosperity of the plant.

What will happen a few weeks after the embryo spike has been removed often surprises the newcomer to delphiniums. New vigorous growth appears from below the soil, and the sight of these fresh shoots is confirmation that your cuttings or seedlings are growing well. In fact, all reputable suppliers of rooted cuttings are reluctant to sell plants until these new growths have appeared, and this explains the reason why specialist growers do not have plants available in early spring. This is something which often annoys the general gardening public, and encourages them to buy undesirable nondescript plants from general gardening centres where they are not looked after so conscientiously.

Plants for early flowering in containers will now be extending their spikes and short stakes will be needed to support the growth. Change the liquid feed to a high potash type, such as those used in tomato growing. Others in pots for normal flowering can have the same treatment and should be left outside from the beginning of the month.

Outside

This is perhaps the delphinium enthusiast's busiest month. Batches of rooted cuttings will need to be planted and the spring-sown seedlings will almost certainly be ready for planting towards the end of the month.

Regular hoeing should be carried out until the end of the month when, if you can afford it, a mulch of organic matter will be of great benefit. It should only be placed in position after heavy rain or after a thorough watering. Almost any organic matter is better than none, although badly-made garden compost which has not heated up during decomposition is doubtful – all you will get is a forest of weeds. This could be a major problem for, as fast as you clear one germination, a fresh crop of weeds will appear. Such material is best left until winter digging is the order of the day. There is little doubt, in my opinion, that bark fibre is the best mulch to use, from a labour-saving point of view. It lasts for some years, allows rain to percolate easily, suppresses weeds extremely well, and does not shift from position even with gale force winds. You can even broadcast soluble fertilisers on its surface, with the certain knowledge that it will be easily washed through to the roots by rain or hose. If the mulch is not for you, then the hoe must be kept going.

Staking

If you intend to grow a fair number of the tall exhibition-type delphiniums, I am ready to admit, contrary to my opening remarks to this calendar, that you will have 'tasks' to carry out. This sort of cultivation can be quite an undertaking if you garden on a very stony or flinty soil, such as is found, for example, in parts of South Buckinghamshire.

Somehow you have to insert 6–9in (15–23cm) of garden cane into the soil, three to a plant, splayed out at an angle away from the stems. This is fairly easy on stoneless soils, especially loams, light clays and sands, for hand and arm pressure is usually sufficient. But I fear that faced with a stony soil you need to be armed with a mallet (a wooden one preferably), for even if you were able to penetrate deeply enough with hand pressure the cane would tend to wander away from the direction needed. Having placed the canes in position the first tie should be made with a loop of the usual garden tying material, and it should be reasonably tight. Canes of about 4ft (120cm) are sufficiently long – as you become more familiar with the habit of various cultivars, you can select those of more appropriate length, the aim being to have a length so that the top of the cane is below the bottom opened floret.

Young plants which were planted out in the previous month must now have the growing point removed, as advocated in March.

Depending on where you live, water may well be needed. This may sound ridiculous to someone who gardens around the west coast of Scotland or in Devon and Cornwall, where the rainfall is high in April, but it should be remembered that, incredible as it may seem, April is on average one of the driest months of the year. Official droughts have sometimes been recorded, but there is no shortage of water in the catchment areas or in reservoirs at this time of the year, so you can water with a clear conscience. Do remember the often-repeated advice – when you water it must be done so that the ground is saturated to a considerable depth. The equivalent of 1in (2.5cm) of rain is not too much. Merely sprinkling the surface probably does more harm than good.

If you intend to enter spikes into competitive classes at flower shows, then some extra feeding should be carried out. With modern soluble fertilisers this is an easy matter, for the powder may be scattered around the plants and watered in. Very few herbaceous plants respond to feeding in the same way as the delphinium. Give the plant a good diet and it will reward you with prodigious growth.

Any cuttings required should be secured now as the growths will soon be too long for this purpose.

MAY

Under Glass

Containers with plants for early flowering will be showing colour by now, and can be placed in position on the patio or terrace. These flowers are a real bonus and are truly worth the effort, for, in addition to having a unique show so early, these plants remain in bloom for much longer than those blooming at the normal time of June and July, simply because the temperature is considerably lower.

Continue to pot up cuttings as they root and place them outside to harden off, which is still necessary even though temperatures are rising. It may be necessary to transfer your set-up for rooting cuttings to a cold frame in a shady position if your glasshouse receives full sun. Temperatures could become excessive with the real chance of too rapid transpiration of unrooted stock.

Outside

This month can be almost as busy as April. Planting of rooted cuttings and seedlings will continue, and particular attention must be given to watering the pots if delay is likely. Even when the seedlings have been planted out you must see that they receive adequate moisture until they are established.

Feeding the plants for exhibition should continue, but an important change is required in the analysis of the feed. Choose one which has been developed for tomato growing as this will contain a much higher proportion of potash. This is important since it assists in hardening the stems, and some growers feel that it also helps to intensify colours.

Staking

A final tie is required, which should be relatively loose, enabling the stems to sway in the wind. If the tie is tight there is a danger of a whiplash effect which can result in a broken spike. If you have been over-generous with the length of your canes then it is a simple matter to remove their tips to below the bottom floret with secateurs.

In early gardens and in some localities, it is possible by now to have the first signs of colour on established plants, in which case no further attention is needed.

Keep a watch for the tell-tale signs of caterpillars which can hide in a curled-up young leaf. Hand picking will give enough control if you only have a few plants, otherwise a spraying with a modern insecticide may be necessary.

Foliar Feeding

If, for one reason or another, you have been unable to find the time to feed your plants, then a foliar feed early on in the month can have beneficial results, particularly if you have flower shows in mind. It is best to choose a proprietary brand specially formulated for this purpose. Due to the large leaf structure of the maturing delphinium, the results of foliar feeding can be very good indeed, and the difference between treated and untreated plants can be quite dramatic.

Seedlings

The main batch of young seedlings is usually ready by now and it is unnecessary to give them more than 12in (30cm) of space each way. This is enough room for them to develop spikes large enough to assess quality and to remove any, even in flower, to a more permanent site.

Rooted Cuttings

The majority of rooted cuttings will now be ready for their final quarters. For ordinary garden purposes 20in (50cm) apart each way is adequate – rather more room should be allowed if you have showing in mind, and 24in (60cm) apart should be regarded as the minimum. A more spacious planting distance is desirable, however, as this does make it so much more easy to attend to the plants' requirements, especially staking.

Laterals

Shortly after the main embryo spike appears and starts to lengthen you will be able to see the emerging laterals. Some enthusiasts will recommend that the top-most ones should be removed. This is a great pity for they do not, in my opinion, deprive the main spike to any great extent of the available food, and I suspect that such growers are devoted exhibitors. These beautiful appendages are so useful in

prolonging the display, and so wonderful for floral arrangements, that my advice is to leave them.

The Chelsea Flower Show

If you can find a spare day, a visit to this show is an
unforgettable experience. You will be able to see some
wonderful delphiniums on the trade stands and, if ever you
wanted confirmation that most of the feeding roots are
contained in the top 12in (30cm), you will find that all the
plants on display are grown in pots no deeper than this. You
may be able to order for immediate delivery or collection at
the nursery any delphiniums which take your fancy, but
such is demand you may also find that some cultivars are
sold out. Do not forget to pay a visit to the Delphinium
Society's stand, where you will find many publications to
assist you and can be told all you want to know about the
flower by the enthusiasts manning it.

JUNE

Under Glass

The glasshouse will now be empty of all matters relating to
the delphinium, so there is plenty of room for tomatoes,
cucumbers, and so on.

Outside

By now all seedlings and rooted cuttings will have been
planted out. Keep pinching out embryo flower spikes on the
rooted cuttings, but let the seedlings run up to flower – to
assist them in their progress an occasional feed is worthwhile. Towards the end of the month some of the most
forward autumn-sown seedlings will possibly be showing
colour, but there will be more on this subject under July.

There is little more to do and you can now just enjoy the
fruits of your labour, unless you plan to exhibit.

Exhibiting

Having read the rules of the Society, one difficulty most
beginners experience is being able to complete an entry form

in advance without knowing for certain if they will have, in pristine condition, the required number of spikes available. In local shows, where there are only a few classes for delphiniums, this is not too much of a problem. But with a national show, especially those held in conjunction with the Royal Horticultural Society, where there can be a score or more classes, more care is needed. As a guide, given average weather conditions, a flower spike will be fully out about four weeks after the embryo spike makes its first appearance. In addition, a spike will be at its best some seven days after the bottom florets begin to open. These guidelines are useful, especially in some cases, where entry forms may be required by the Secretary fourteen days before the show.

Selection

Never choose a spike which is past its best, for it will only deteriorate even more quickly after cutting. Always choose a specimen which is nearing its best, even though it may be smaller, with a number of unopened florets at the top.

Cutting

This can be something of a lottery – if you decide to cut on the morning of the show, and there has been rain overnight, you will be in real trouble if the show is any distance away. If it is a local show, within walking distance and the blooms can be carried, then all will be well, but if they have to be packed into the average car then, I fear, they are unlikely to be worth putting on the show bench. On the other hand, if the blooms have remained dry and have been able to enjoy cooler conditions overnight, then they will be fully charged with the maximum moisture content from the root system. On balance, it is safer to cut the evening before the show and to place the blooms in water under cover, unless you have more faith in weather forecasts than I do. (*See* Chapter 8 for more information on showing.)

JULY

Under Glass

Hybridisation

In some years it is difficult to find pollen from a selected parent due to constant rain, which not only tends to wash the pollen away, but also creates a situation where pollination is impossible. This is particularly a problem for those gardeners who are away at work all day, and a situation can easily arise where the receptive pistil passes the stage whereby it can accept pollen. There is, however, a way in which you can always have ripe pollen available, and that is to carry out hybridisation on laterals. If laterals are cut when they are partially open, and placed in water in a glasshouse, the rain and wind will have no effect and as a result you will have plenty of pollen at any time. There is a good case in any event for using laterals as it means you need not disfigure the main spike, and for most gardeners a few pods on a lateral will yield all the seed they are likely to be able to deal with.

There are even some devoted amateurs who grow selected plants in pots and transfer both parents from outside to the glasshouse so that the procedure for making a cross is completely under control. This system is pretty foolproof and is in fact practised by Dr Legro with his 'university hybrids'.

OUTSIDE

In late gardens the main display will be at its best in July, and even those situated in more favourable areas will still have plenty of colour.

This is a good time to visit other venues where delphiniums are a speciality, and the Delphinium Society publishes a list of gardens where delphiniums dominate and visitors are welcome. This service is really for members, but I am sure that if you were to make discreet enquiries with the Secretary he would be prepared to supply the name and address of a garden near you which you could visit, providing suitable enquiries were made to the owner first.

Perhaps the best place to visit is the trial ground of the Royal Horticultural Society at Wisley. Here you will be able to see at least 100, and probably more, different cultivars, including the most up-to-date, as well as new seedlings selected for trial. There is no better place to see all the finest plants growing together, and you can be sure that you will be able to select the names of those plants which you fancy, and whose habit and growth may suit your own purposes better than others.

Cuttings

Continue to pinch out any embryo flower spikes on late-struck cuttings. If you were able to secure early cuttings from stools taken into a glasshouse, these plants will now be growing vigorously. They will have produced one or more shoots from below the soil surface, if you have followed the advice to pinch out the embryo spikes at the first opportunity. Allow one shoot to develop and run up to flower. This is one way of having blooms out of season, for a spike will be produced which will be fully out in late summer or the early autumn.

Seedlings

Growing delphiniums from seed can become quite addictive, especially if the seed has been produced from your own hand-crosses. Those who have experienced even a modest trial of, say, twenty to thirty plants will admit that the anticipation of inspecting the seedlings as they open for the first time is unlike any other gardening activity. With a good choice of parents, hand-crossed seed will produce exceedingly good offspring, and those gardeners who are new to this exciting part of delphinium growing can all too easily fall into the trap of considering that most of them are of sufficient merit to retain. This is a mistake. However good they may seem at first glance, you must examine them objectively, and ruthlessly discard those which are not comparable with modern named cultivars. Any which are considered to be promising and are worthy of being retained for another year can be removed to a more permanent site. This may sound surprising, but these young plants *are* capable of being transplanted, even in full flower, as long as you are careful to retain a good ball of soil around the root system and to water them well when they are in their new site. This economic use of a site for seedlings makes sense, for those discarded can be removed and burnt (after cutting the spikes for arrangement), and the area will then become vacant for yet another trial. At the same time it gives you the time to clean up the area and to cultivate the soil for the next batch of seedlings which can be planted in the autumn. (*See* August and October.)

AUGUST

Outside

The main display will now be past its best and you should start to remove the actual flower spikes and laterals if these too have finished flowering. It is important to retain the foliage in order to avoid forcing the plants to flower again. It sometimes happens, especially with certain plants, that new growth will appear in any event. By all means in those cases remove all old growth to ground level and allow the secondary spikes to develop and flower. If you intend to replace the plants then by all means cut them down to ground level at the first opportunity, give them a liberal dressing of a general fertiliser and water well.

Seed Harvest

Towards the end of the month the seed pods will start to change in colour from green to brown. Before they turn to a deep brown they should be removed in order to prevent loss as they mature and, especially in the case of hand crosses, to stop members of the finch family from devouring your endeavours. If the seed is sown straight away, it will germinate as fast as 'mustard and cress' and, perhaps more importantly, the resultant seedlings will provide plants large enough to be planted out in a prepared site – this might be one left vacant from a previous seed trial. Any seed not sown must be stored in your refrigerator.

The first of the spring-sown seedlings will start to bloom towards the end of the month, and they should be subjected to the same analysis as outlined for autumn-sown plants.

All plants which are to remain *in situ* to bloom the following year should be given a thorough watering in times of low rainfall. This will assist in building up the dormant eyes, which start to develop below ground when flowering has ceased and from which the following year's shoots arise.

Should mildew become a nuisance one spray with a modern systemic fungicide will usually be sufficient, and it is a good plan to give a similar spray to young seedlings on the basis that prevention is better than cure.

SEPTEMBER

Spring-sown seedlings will now be giving of their best. It needs to be stressed, especially to beginners, that you should harden your heart and be ruthless with selection.

Rooted cuttings will now start to throw strong, fresh growth from below soil level. These should be allowed to develop, but, unless you are prepared to accept a reduced performance the following year, you should only allow a few bottom florets to remain, pinching out the rest of the spike as soon as it is large enough to handle. On the other hand, if you had in mind an autumn display, and perhaps aimed to enter flower competitions, you should feed these rooted cuttings well and ensure they receive an abundance of water – you will have a superb display lasting well into the following month. Properly grown, these young spikes can be on a par with those which flower at the normal time. I can promise that, if you do enter flower competitions, you can cause quite a sensation and people will wonder how you managed to produce delphiniums so late in the year.

Seed sown last month will be ready for transplanting on to a 3in (7.5cm) pot in well-enriched compost.

OCTOBER

Spring-planted rooted cuttings and plants from spring-sown seed will still be giving a fine show if you have allowed them to bloom. Towards the end of the month, as daylight diminishes, there will be a steady decrease in growth on all plants – the bonus will come from the longer-lasting qualities of those in flower.

If you are unable to sow seed until well after the harvesting time, then the resultant seedlings will not have developed sufficiently for planting out and are best left in their 3in (7.5cm) pots to die down naturally. To this end a cold frame can be useful – not because the plants need protection from the winter, for they are completely hardy, but rather because they need to shelter from excessive rain. You must ensure that anti–slug treatment keeps the frame free of these pests.

NOVEMBER

As with most gardening, November is the month to tidy up. All canes should be pulled up, plants should be cut down to soil level and all debris removed. For those gardeners who are reluctant, for their own ecological reasons (and one must respect their views), to use chemical control of slugs, one reasonably successful method is to remove the soil carefully from around the crown of the plants and to replace this with coarse, sharp sand. This is an old-fashioned method and it can work . The action of worms and other beneficial insects will tend to distribute the dressing about the surrounding soil after a while, and for this method to be effective the sand should be replenished from time to time. It is astonishing how worm activity can leave no trace of the sharp sand by the following spring, leaving the plants vulnerable to attack. For those with no inhibitions against chemical control, now is a good time, as you are tidying up the area, to apply a watering of aluminum sulphate at 2oz/1 gallon (about 6g/ 9 litres), using this amount to roughly 4 sq yd (less than 1 sq m).

DECEMBER

Those with a moderately heated glasshouse can bring in the pots containing young seedlings from sowings made in the autumn, in order to give them a head start. No attempt should be made to force them (unless you are prepared to give additional light by using horticultural fluorescent tubes), otherwise poor spindly growth will be the result. The ideal temperature for them is a few degrees above freezing.

Apart from the above, the best advice is to take things easy – in a few short weeks there will be more than enough to keep you busy on the road to successful and rewarding delphinium cultivation.

11

Garden Design

The design of a garden often reflects not only the personality of the gardener, but, along with the manner in which the plants (including delphiniums) are grown, can usually also indicate the purpose behind all the endeavour of this most popular of all British hobbies. The aims and aspirations of gardeners differ widely. This is a blessing (as indeed it is in all other human activities), as otherwise we would end up with all gardens following a similar pattern – to say the least this would be extremely uninteresting.

During a lifetime of visiting other people's gardens where delphiniums are grown – sometimes almost to the exclusion of all other plants, but more often than not as part of a broad spectrum of plants – I have seen so many variations that I feel qualified to mention in general terms the main differences. The reader should adapt those aspects he likes, in order for the design to fit in with his or her own particular requirements, or desires.

MOVING TO A NEW GARDEN

Most of us have been, or will be, faced at some time with a move from one house to another. The contents of a house are an easy matter, best left to the removal firm, but dealing with the contents of a garden is not so simple. In general terms it seems that the contents of a garden belong to the purchaser, unless arrangements are made with regard to specified items. Fortunately, the usual delay involved in moving is one aspect which can actually work to your advantage so far as the delphinium is concerned.

Taking Cuttings

Once it is established, the delphinium resents disturbance. A mature delphinium will seldom recover from being transplanted, so there is no need to make any arrangements with your buyer to remove established plants. If you plan to move before the spring, then all you need to do is to obtain permission from the new owner of your house to visit the garden in the spring to take cuttings from the established plants. This has worked well in several cases known to me – the new owners have in all cases been very co-operative, showing considerable interest in this aspect of propagation. If however, the move is to take place at another time the situation is much simpler. You can choose either to take cuttings in the spring or, if you are too late for this, you can have recourse to taking eye cuttings in the summer. Once rooted the cuttings from either method are potted up progressively, until they can finally be placed in large containers should the move become protracted. There is no need to use expensive pots for the final potting – cheap and easily obtainable black polythene containers, which open up to 10–12in (25–30cm), are perfectly satisfactory for at least twelve months.

It may well be that your new garden is an established one, in which case it may be best to treat your containerised delphiniums as stock plants and to propagate from the crowns in the following year. This will allow you sufficient time to make any alterations to the design of your new garden and to prepare the site thoroughly. On the other hand you may be lucky and have, for example, a vegetable plot which would be absolutely ideal to receive your delphinium plants. Not only would you be able to have a display of spikes, but also the plants would be all the better for propagation purposes the following year, leaving you with plenty of time to use the vegetable plot for its proper purpose. Your task is, of course, made much simpler if the garden is a new one, for the containerised plants can be settled into any odd corner, or even in a permanent site if time permits.

Using Seed

Plants from seed should not be overlooked as a means of providing a spectacular display in your new garden and to this end my own experiences are worth recalling. Some thirty years ago I was faced with a move to a newly-built house on a vacant plot. Circumstances prevented me from being able to obtain cuttings from named cultivars in my old garden, so instead I obtained a variety of hand-crossed seed from various sources. This was sown in the summer of the year of the move which took place in the following February. The 300 or so seedlings had made sufficient growth to be moved to 5in (12.5cm) pots, where they remained until they were duly moved, together with our household effects. A strip of ground was rotavated by a contractor in a part of the garden which I had set aside as being suitable for a hardy plant border. A soil analysis revealed that the soil was very fertile – hardly surprising, for it had been used for grazing purposes for many years. With no further soil preparation (other than a consolidation by treading) the young plants, which had started into growth, were planted out from their 5in pots in late March, 30in (75cm) apart each way. After planting each delphinium received a dressing of dried blood at the rate of 3oz to the square yard (about 9g to the square metre). Weeds were a problem but very frequent hoeing kept them under reasonable control. The seedlings grew at a prodigious rate and it was obvious that in most cases I could allow two or even three spikes to flower per plant. It happened to be a favourable spring and early summer from the delphiniums point of view and, at the risk of sounding immodest, the sight of around 700 of these seedlings caused a minor sensation with neighbours and those out walking – in the garden, which was devoid of any screening, they were visible from quite a long distance.

To the absolute astonishment of my friends and fellow competitors in the Delphinium Society, I was even able to enter the whole section for seedling classes in the London show in the July. Even more surprising was the fact that I won the trophy for the highest number of points in the classes for seedlings raised by an exhibitor. I mention this moment of personal satisfaction not, I hope, sounding boastful, but in order to illustrate how relatively easy it is to provide a most worthwhile display at a minimum expense. It is sad to relate that none of the seedlings were of sufficient merit to keep, except for two, which did, after several generations of crossing, provide me with plants of a sufficiently good quality to be named and registered with the Royal Horticultural Society.

HAVING A PLANTING SCHEME

That was one approach to delphiniums in the garden. To many, however, the very idea of a massed planting of one genus is anathema, while to others the thought of cutting the blooms for the show bench, thus depriving the garden of display, is seen as callous. There are also gardeners who despise that dedicated band of enthusiasts who delight in the artistic interpretation of flowers and foliage in the form of arrangements. Thank goodness all gardeners are not of the same persuasion. However, it does seem to me that the majority share a love for the garden as a whole, with the delphinium playing its part in a mixed planting and design which leads to an effect that is pleasantly harmonious. Regimented rows of delphiniums, spaced especially for ease of cultivation, favoured by the real plantsman, the exhibitor, and sometimes the floral arranger, are not for this type of gardener.

Assuming that you are all lovers of the genus, it is useful to consider how the delphinium can fit into a general planting scheme. The actual design of a garden is a personal matter, and yet it must be admitted that some people are unable to achieve a result which is satisfactory even to themselves. An artistic sense is something of a gift, and there are those who know what they want in a design but who are incapable of achieving it. You should beware of dogmatic statements on design, but there are well-proven examples where experience in this field suggests basic principles which are common to all successful gardens.

The background is possibly the most important feature to bear in mind before planting delphiniums, closely followed by the foreground which must also be considered very seriously. There is nothing worse than the forlorn sight of browning foliage and stems in late summer and early autumn from delphiniums which have ceased their flowering period.

It is hard to improve on a background which is predominantly green. A hedge, or a mixture of shrubs and trees, is ideal, as long as you take care to see that the roots of the delphinium are not too close to competing roots. This type of background can also provide a bonus if the delphiniums are planted to the leeward side of prevailing winds, as the filtered effect will give the best possible protection against breakage on an exposed site. The alternative to green is the sky itself, making sure that the darker colours are at the back of the planting. In this case, if the site is one which receives strong winds, care must be taken to plant only those delphiniums which are known to produce wind-resistant spikes.

Your choice of plants should be restricted to such cultivars as 'Mighty Atom', 'Lord Butler', 'Clack's Choice', 'Charles G Broan', 'Loch Nevis' and 'Loch Leven'. These will give you a good colour range of purples and blues, and if you add 'Claire' you can have a short dusky-pink as well. I am sad to say that I cannot recommend any white delphinium able to withstand summer gales and storms without fracturing when planted in a very exposed position.

Most flowers look their best when they are planted in bold groups rather than on their own as isolated specimens. The delphinium is no different, and groups of three of the same cultivar always seem to succeed.

The hardest part of design is how to screen the dying foliage. This needs to be accomplished by mid-August, especially when you are considering a mixed hardy plant border. One of the most accommodating plants which fills this role is achillea. The cultivar 'Gold Plate' is the best – apart from its stiff, erect foliage which does not require staking, the huge heads of gold will hide the 'spent' delphiniums extremely well. Later to bloom but also with sufficient foliage to do the job is the Michaelmas daisy (perennial aster). Again, no staking will be required. Of course, there is nothing to stop you using annuals in front of the delphiniums, and I have seen splendid dahlias serving a screening purpose in more than one delphinium garden.

I don't think I would be contradicted if I said that the most universally admired flower is the rose and there are few gardens that don't have some. There are a number of schemes where the rose and the delphinium are grown together in quantity and, as they bloom at practically the same time, you can imagine what a splendid combination they can make. One of the most delightful ways of associating the two is to grow climbers and ramblers on pergolas as a background, and for the border itself to choose from the many shrub roses which are returning to favour.

THE ONE-COLOUR BORDER

A really stunning show can be created by using only blue-coloured delphiniums along with other flowers of a similar colour. The choice is not great but there are several gems. My first choice for the front is the beautiful hardy penstemon 'Blue Gem' which has erect stems of approximately 18in

(45cm) and clusters of the most lovely clear mid–blue flowers. A little further back can be planted the true geranium, which is of course hardy – the cultivar 'Johnson Blue' is hard to beat. There are several veronicas which are true blue and perhaps the cultivar 'Shirley Blue' is the best for your purpose. Suitable for the middle and the back of the border, there is a huge range of campanulas in various shades of blue. *C. pyramidalis* is the tallest of the campanulas, growing up to 6ft (180cm), and its blue shades are a perfect foil for the delphinium. A somewhat shorter plant is *C. lactiflora*, of which 'Pritchards Variety' and 'Pouffe' are two reliable blue cultivars. *C. carpatica* is a very short, sprawling plant, suitable for the edge of the border where it can tumble down, perhaps to soften a stone path – 'Ditton Blue' is the most popular cultivar.

THE WHITE BORDER

I have seen two superb examples of a border containing only white flowers – in one, silver foliage has been included, which adds greatly to the end result. There are three outstanding white delphiniums – 'Sandpiper' with a deep brown eye, 'Olive Poppleton', with a honey-coloured eye and (a fairly recent introduction) 'Shasta', with a pure black eye. Fortunately, the choice of white flowers to act as companions to the delphiniums is wide-ranging. Again, campanula is available in a variety of heights, all bearing white flowers. *C. lactiflora* grows to 1–5ft (30–150cm) and its white flowers are borne in clusters – 'Alba' is the best white form. A shorter species, *C. persicifolia*, can be obtained in white and is useful for the front of the border.

The garden pink is almost indispensable for the white border, and the white 'Mrs Simkins' is so well known and so easily grown that it requires no introduction. Its strong perfume is an undeniable asset and its silver foliage will blend well. But perhaps the most striking combination of plants can be had by planting the white delphinium with white lilies. *L. candidum*, better known as the 'Madonna Lily', will bloom at the same time as the earliest delphiniums, whereas *L. regale* will bloom with the late delphiniums. There are two other notable lilies bearing pure white flowers – *L. princeps* and *L. speciosum* – which will still be in flower as the last delphiniums begin to fade.

THE ISLAND SITE

In contrast to the border (which, by definition, means a flower-bed to one side of a garden, more often than not against the boundary of the property), an island site is usually surrounded by a lawn and can thus be viewed from any angle. There is much to be said for such a site, particularly in today's small gardens for, providing it is not too wide, it can be cultivated without you needing to tread on the soil once planting has been completed. Comments made concerning the border apply equally well to the island site, so you can easily have mixed hardy perennials. If you have formed a liking for plants such as the dahlia or the chrysanthemum to a degree where you would like to specialise in one or both as well as in the delphinium, I can think of no more delightful or convenient way of growing them together. The delphiniums should be planted in the centre of the island, leaving sufficient space around the perimeter for the other flower of your choice in a double staggered line. The advantage of such an arrangement will soon become obvious when the dahlias or chrysanthemums are lifted after the first frosts. You can then gain access to the delphiniums in order to cut them down to ground level, remove the stakes, tidy up the ground and apply anti-slug precautions. When spring comes around, feeding, taking of cuttings *in situ*, and staking and tying can all be accomplished long before the time arrives to plant the dahlias or chrysanthemums. When the delphiniums are at their peak their bed-mates will still be small, allowing the magnificent spikes to be viewed from any part of the garden. As the weeks pass the delphiniums will begin to fade, and by the end of July they will be starting to die down naturally. It is at this stage that you will appreciate the masking qualities provided by the foliage of other plants. With early chrysanthemums or dahlias the expanding growth can easily be attended to from the edge of the lawn, together with staking, tying and disbudding. Soon all vestiges of the dying foliage of the delphiniums will be hidden from view, leaving you with the delights of the flowers from the companion plants.

THE VEGETABLE PLOT

There comes a time, as you grow older, when the vegetable garden no longer seems so desirable. This may arise because finances become easier, or because children have grown up and married and moved away, leaving less mouths to feed. Or it may be because you decide you want to grow more flowers, and to avoid the undoubted intensive labour required to grow vegetables successfully. The rectangular plot usually devoted to vegetables is often at the end of the garden, secluded because of other design features. Here you have the perfect site for growing delphiniums, as well as other flowers, for cutting for the house and, if it takes your fancy, for exhibition.

With the well-cultivated soil it is difficult to envisage a better site for a large trial of delphiniums from seed, where the plants can be grown in regimented rows to facilitate cultivation (*see* Chapter 3). On this plot you should also have room to plant named cultivars for stock purposes, and somewhere to stand those container-grown plants used to decorate the patio – both before they are in bloom and once they have passed their best. You may also welcome the additional space which will enable you to erect a glasshouse, or cold frame or two, which can help enormously in contributing to the successful growing of delphiniums, especially if you do become something of an enthusiast.

RUNNING OUT OF SPACE

Sometimes (and not infrequently), the interest in producing your own delphiniums from crosses leads to a shortage of space. This was not much of a problem in the past, when the vast majority of housing developments were built on plots of a reasonable size. Land was also relatively cheap and it was a fairly inexpensive matter to purchase a large plot on which to build the house of your choice. The position today is significantly different. In new developments quite substantial houses are built on plots so small that the gardens should really be termed 'back yards'. So what can you do if your interest has developed to such an extent that you literally have no room left to expand? One obvious way is to move house to a property which has a more spacious garden. For a number of reasons this solution will be feasible for few families, although one young enthusiast of my acquaintance has taken the drastic step of changing his job location from the expensive South-east to the Midlands, in order to be able to afford the size of garden that he needs to fulfil his aspirations. It would be foolish to suggest that this is a viable alternative for the vast majority, but there is increasing evidence that quality of life can be as important as career prospects to many young people.

One leading delphinium enthusiast has found a solution which has proved to be most satisfactory. His neighbours are elderly folk who found that the maintenance of their garden was becoming increasingly difficult. Being garden lovers, they were in despair at their beautifully-designed plot becoming neglected, so an agreement was reached. Part of the garden is maintained by our enthusiast, on condition that only delphinium seedlings will be grown. This area was formerly the kitchen garden and was in bad repair – now it is the home of hundreds of delphinium seedlings, giving great enjoyment to the owners and at the same time solving the problem of the keen grower.

There was a time only a few years ago when allotments were in great demand but, with the changing patterns of the supply of really fresh organically-grown vegetables, this has fallen considerably. Several enthusiasts have taken advantage of this change and now grow substantial quantities of seedlings for trial on allotments.

12

Species and Cultivars

SPECIES

There are several hundred recorded species scattered throughout the world and there are, no doubt, many more which have not been satisfactorily noted by botanists. One great difficulty in listing species is to be accurate, for many known synonyms exist. There is the distinct possibility that over-zealous botanists during the Victorian period, when so much 'plant hunting' was carried out, have labelled identical wild delphiniums with different names, simply because the discovery was made at about the same time but by two or more botanists. Some descriptions by authorities in the past have to be questioned, for it has been found that when the plants have flowered, some features mentioned are far removed from the results. Errors have been compounded by authors of books on the delphinium to such an extent that even colours quoted of particular species vary.

To unravel this unsatisfactory position would probably take a lifetime of research and would certainly require visits to the many areas of the world where species exist. One has to face facts that such a research programme is most unlikely ever to receive sponsorship and the family fortunes which during Victorian times enabled the younger members to travel far and wide, no longer exist.

It is for this reason that I feel obliged to limit this list to those species which I feel are authentic, and which have been flowered by reliable plantsmen away from their natural habitat.

Name	Description	Origin
D. ajacis	The larkspur – blue, 3ft (90cm)	Europe, including United Kingdom
D. alpestre	Mid-blue, yellow eye, 8in (20cm)	Colorado, USA
D. altissimum	Blue to purple, 3ft (90cm)	High in the Himalyas
D. andersonii	Blue and purple, 3ft (90cm)	Columbia, USA

122

D. astaphisagria	Red/purple, height uncertain. Poisonous	Southern Europe
D. atropurpureum	See *D. cashmirianum*	
D. aurantiacum	A variety of *D. nudicaule*	
D. alureum	Light blue, 2–3ft (60–90cm)	Rocky Mountains, USA
D. biternatum	Similar to *D. zalil*	Turkestan
D. brunonianum	Purple/violet, 12in (30cm). Musk scent	Himalayas
D. burkii	Indigo, 2ft (60cm)	California, USA
D. candidum	See *D. leroyi*	
D. cardinale	Scarlet, 6–8ft (180–240cm)	California, USA
D. cardiopetalum	Blue/purple, 12in (30cm), annual	Mediterranean
D. carolinium	Blue, 2ft (60cm)	N. Carolina, USA
D. carporum	White and pink, 12in (30cm)	W. Rocky Mountains, USA
D. cashmeriana (also *D. cashmiriana* and *D. cashmirianum*	Deep blue, light blue, light purple, dark purple and variations, 12in (30cm)	Kashmir and Himalayas
D. catsienense	See *D. tatsienense*	
D. caucasicum	Purple, white eye, 4in (10cm)	Caucasus
D. cheilanthum	Dark blue, 3ft (90cm)	Siberia
D. chinensis and *D. chinense*	Synonymous with *D. grandiflorum*	
D. cockerelli	Metallic purple, 4ft (120cm)	S. Colorado, USA
D. coelestinum	Azure blue, 4ft (120cm)	E. Szechuan
D. coeruleum	Light blue, 12in (30cm)	Sikkim and Tibet
D. consolida	The branching larkspur. Height various, colour various. Much hybridised	Europe and now the UK
D. dasycarpum	Light blue, 4–6ft (120–180cm). Could be identical to *D. elatum* and not a separate species	Caucasus
D. davidii	Deep blue, 3ft (90cm)	E. Tibet
D. decorum	Blue or violet, 18in (45cm)	California and possibly Russia
D. devaricatum (also probably *D. divaricatum*)	Blue – height uncertain	Caspian, Iran and Caucasus
D. dictyocarpum (also probably *D. dyctyscarpum*)	Pale blue, 2ft (60cm)	Caucasus and Siberia
D. distichum	Pale blue, tall	Rocky Mountains, USA

D. duhmbergii	White or blue, 6ft (180cm)	Russia
D. elatum	Cornflower blue, 6ft (180cm) (Almost universally accepted as being one of the parents of modern hybrids.)	Swiss Alps
D. elegans	Blue, 18in (45cm)	USA
D. emiliae	Blue shades, 12in (30cm)	W. California, USA
D. exaltatum	Much confusion exists – could be the *D. elatum* of the USA	W. California, USA
D. fargesii	Blue, 1ft (30cm)	Szechuan
D. fissum	Blue, 3ft (90cm)	Hungary
D. formosum	Violet/blue, 2–3ft (60–90cm) (This could be *D. elatum?*)	Swiss Alps.
D. freynii	Bright blue, 12in (30cm)	Caucasus
D. geraniifolium	Dark blue, 12in (30cm)	Rocky Mountains, USA
D. geyeri	Azure blue, 18in (45cm). Very poisonous	Rocky Mountains and Colorado, USA
D. grandiflorum (Synonymous with *D. chinensis, D. chinense,* and *D. sinense*)	Various colours, 2ft (60cm). Much hybridised, leading to many named cultivars including 'Blue Butterfly', 'Blue Gem' and 'Azure Fairy'	Russia, China and Siberia
D. hansenii	Pinky mauve, 2ft (60cm)	California, USA
D. hesperium	Clear blue, 2ft (60cm) (could this be the same as *D. hansenii?*)	California, USA
D. hillcoatiae	White, tinged with green – height unknown	Tibet
D. hybidum	Blue and white, 3ft (90cm)	Turkestan and Siberia
D. laxiflorum	Pale blue, 12in (30cm)	Altai Mountains and Siberia
D. leptophyllum	Deep blue – Height unknown	Mexico
D. leroyi	Pale blue, scented, 3ft (90cm) *D. candidum* is synonymous with *D. leroyi* in respect of a scented white variation.)	Kenya and Uganda
D. likiangense	Gentian blue, scent of hyacinth, 12in (30cm)	Yunnan and N. China
D. luteum	Yellow form of *D. nudicaule*	California, USA
D. menzesii (*D. menziesii*)	Mid-blue, 12in (30cm)	California and W. Coast of USA

Species and Cultivars

Species	Description	Origin
D. nanum	Blue, height unknown	Egypt
D. nelsonii	Blue, 6in (15cm)	Nebraska, USA
D. nudicaule	Vermilion scarlet, 18in (45cm). Variations include yellow	Oregon, San Francisco, California, USA
D. ochroleucum	Lemon, 2ft (60cm)	Caucasus, Iberia, Georgia, Turkestan, Siberia, China
D. orientale	Purple, 3ft (90cm) (A dried specimen is said to have been found in the tomb of King Ahmes which still retained its colour from entombment around 1700 BC)	Turkestan
D. orthocentron	Pale blue, 18in (45cm)	Sutcheun
D. oxypetalium	Pale blue, 12in (30cm)	Central Europe
D. parishii	Blue, 18in (45cm)	California, USA
D. parryi	Deep blue, 2ft (60cm)	California, USA
D. penhardii	A white form of D. carolinium	California, USA
D. przewaldskii	Pale yellow, tipped blue, 12–24in (30–60cm)	Mongolia
D. requieni	Blue/white, with pink and green marks, 2–3ft (60–90cm)	S. W. Europe and Majorca
D. scaposum	Dark blue, leafless, 2ft (60cm)	S. Rockies, USA
D. scorpulorum	Similar to D. elatum, 4ft (120cm)	California, USA
D. simplex	Blue with white eye, 2–3ft (60–90cm)	Idaho and Oregon Mountains
D. staphisagria	Purple – florets resemble a lupin. Poisonous. 2–3ft (60–90cm). One of the earliest delphiniums to be recorded – 1596	Southern Europe
D. tanguiticum	Violet blue, white eye, 4in (10cm)	Kansu and Szechuan
D. tatienense (or D, tatsiense or D. tatsienense (or D. tatsuense)	Cornflower blue, 12–18in (30–45cm)	Szechuan
D. tibeticum	Deep blue, 2ft (60cm)	Tibet
D. tricorne	Blue, white eye, poisonous, 9in (20cm)	North America (Atlantic coast)
D. triste	Mahogany red, spurs violet, 12–24in (30–60cm)	Siberia
D. trollifolium	Dark blue, white eye, 12in (30cm)	Columbia River Valley, USA

D. tsarongense	Blue/green, scented, 18in (45cm)	Armenia and Chinese Alps
D. vestitum	Violet, 4–5ft (120–150cm)	Himalayas, Pakistan, Afghanistan, China
D. vimineum	Azure, probably a form of *D. carolinium*	
D. welbeyi (or *D. welbyi* or *D. wellbeyi* or *D. wellbyi*)	Blue/mauve scented 3ft (90cm)	Ethiopia
D. yunnanens (or *D. yunnanense*)	Blue, brown eye, 2ft (60cm)	China, Tibet
D. zalil	Vivid yellow – sometimes with orange tip, 3–4ft (90–120cm)	Afghanistan, Iran

OTHER HYBRIDS OR STRAINS

Belladonnas

A distinct race having forty-eight chromosomes and single florets. They are seldom grown today and are rarely available from commercial sources.

Connecticut Yankees

Raised by Edward Steichen from the USA. The true strain produces bushy plants of around 3ft (90cm) overall height, and the colour range is quite extensive. The single florets tend to shatter but this is compensated by the ability of the plant to produce several flushes of bloom. This variety is not very perennial in Britain. Some strains offered for sale produce plants with spikes of up to 6ft (180cm) overall and are clearly not the original strain.

University Hybrids

See Chapter 1.

SOME RECOMMENDED NAMED CULTIVARS

There have been many hundreds of named delphiniums commercially available over the years. Many have been superceded by better cultivars of similar colour and habit, while other older delphiniums have deteriorated and stocks of vigorous plants of their type no longer exist. All the plants in the following list are reliable and generally available. All have been registered and most have received awards after trial by the Royal Horticultural Society at Wisley.

Code

(E) Early
(M) Mid-season
(L) Late
(Ex) Good for exhibition
(S) Short
(A) Average Height
(T) Tall

Alice Artindale (E, A)   A rarity in delphiniums for it has fully double blooms, known as 'ranunculas'. Bi-colour of rosy-mauve tinged with sky-blue markings. A very old cultivar raised in 1935. Stocks are variable and great care is needed with selection. Prone to mildew. When at its best it is a fine cut flower.

Aphrodite (M, A)   Pale pink, almost double. Very vigorous producing strong stems.

Blue Nile (M, S, Ex)   Perhaps the purest mid-blue available with little or no other colour in the petals. A contrasting white eye adds to its appeal.

Bruce (M, T, Ex)   Deep violet purple with a greyish-brown eye. As with most purples, can be prone to mildew. This cultivar can produce huge spikes and is a consistent winner at the major flower shows.

Butterball (M, A, Ex)   Deep cream with a bright yellow eye giving an overall appearance close to pale yellow. As with all the so-called 'yellow' cultivars, constitution is not of the highest order. It needs to be propagated frequently in order to maintain vigour.

Charles Gregory Broan (M, S)   Of the clearest pale blue, it has a neat white eye. Being very short in habit it is to be highly recommended for windswept sites. A good garden plant.

Chelsea Star (M, T, Ex)   A rich velvety royal purple, with a pure white contrasting eye. Very large florets of beautiful shape. When well grown it is universally acclaimed as one of the most lovely modern cultivars. It is prone to mildew, and stocks are variable, giving rise in some cases to poor performance, thus great care is needed with selection.

Clack's Choice (M, S)   Pale blue, dark eye. An extremely good garden plant requiring only a minimum of staking. A mature plant can produce as many as twenty short spikes, emminently suitable for floral decoration.

Claire (M, S)   Pale pink with a pinkish-white eye. Strong stems are a feature as well as the ability to hold the bottom florets until the whole spike is fully open. A good garden cultivar.

Cream Cracker (M, A, Ex)   Overall appearance is yellow. Vivid yellow eye. Needs to be propagated frequently to maintain vigour, as is the case with all yellowish cultivars.

Emily Hawkins (M, T, Ex)   Pale violet tinged with blue. Superb form and a vigorous plant. Although a consistent winner on the show bench, it is fine for garden purposes as it will produce many spikes suitable for cutting.

Fanfare (E, T, Ex)   Silvery pastel mauve. Although introduced many years ago this cultivar has retained its vigour. Exceptionally early and a sure winner on the show bench.

Faust (M, T)   Unique ultramarine with an inconspicuous eye of indigo. A good garden plant.

128

Fenella (M, A) Introduced at the same time as 'Blue Nile'. The colour is wonderful, being a true gentian blue with a deep black eye.

Gillian Dallas (L, A, Ex) A really handsome plant. It has unusual colours best described as slate blue-grey. The white eye contrasts well. Can be grown to an enormous size, but loses none of its almost perfect shape. A very late cultivar.

Gordon Forsyth (M, T, Ex) Pure amethyst, small dark eye. Of fine form, it can be prone to mildew. It is perhaps losing some of its vigour, but has such an unusual colour that it is still worth a place.

Gossamer (M, A, Ex) *See* 'Spindrift', to which this is similar, although not as green and also somewhat paler.

Guy Langdon (M/L, T, Ex) Plum-purple, striped eye. Essential to obtain a good clone, as there are some poor plants in cultivation.

Hilda Lucas (L, T, Ex) Mainly mid-blue, but tinged pinkish-mauve. An astonishing plant which has retained its vigour although introduced many years ago. A long-lived plant in any soil, its exhibition-sized spikes are sure winners on the show bench. Of beautiful form, this outstanding cultivar is probably the last of all delphiniums to bloom.

Loch Leven (M, S, Ex) Light blue with a white eye.

Loch Lomond (M, T, Ex) Rich blue with a white eye.

Loch Nevis (E, T, Ex) Light blue with a white eye. Poor-shaped floret. For about ten years it was a consistent winner of the highest awards at the Royal Horticultural Society's shows in London. There is evidence that some loss of vigour is taking place, but it is worth growing especially if a good clone can be obtained.

Lord Butler (M, S) Pale Cambridge blue with a white eye. A very vigorous true short plant, growing to no more than 4ft (120cm) overall. Easy to propagate.

Mighty Atom (L, S, Ex) Deep lavender – double in appearance. Very vigorous. Extremely late. Quite short overall.

Morning Cloud (M, A) A pretty pale blue, flushed slightly pink. A good garden plant.

Nimrod (M, T) A rather narrow spike, but of a royal purple colour. Very tall and vigorous.

Olive Poppleton (M, T, Ex) A unique delphinium. Off-white with a large, glowing honey eye. Much used by plant breeders, it should be in everyone's collection.

Pericles (M, A) Soft mid-blue. A fine garden plant of a true blue tone without a trace of any other colour.

Rosemary Brock (M, A) Dusky pink with brown eye.

Royal Flush (M, T, Ex) Dusky-pink, large florets. Perhaps the most vigorous in the colour range. Capable of producing large spikes of fine substance. Overall length is shorter than most dusky-pinks.

Sabu (M, T, Ex) The darkest of all the purples with a dark eye. Not a very long-lived plant and should be propagated annually. Reliable stock is scarce, but 'Sabu' has been included as it can produce immense spikes.

Sandpiper (E, T, Ex) Probably the best of the whites, a fine black eye. Indispensable for exhibition.

Sarah Edwards (M, A) Mid-violet, white eye. Good garden cultivar.

Skyline (L, M) Pure sky-blue with a white eye. This lovely, very late delphinium has an almost double appearance. Not very long-lived and should be propagated frequently.

Spindrift (M, A, Ex) A most unusual cultivar. In some seasons and on some soils it produces florets of a turquoise colour, intermingled with soft blues and pinks. Highly regarded by devotees of floral art. It is also an extremely good exhibition plant.

Summerfield Miranda (E/M, A)   Pale pink with brown eye.

Summer Haze (M, A)   Pale lavender blue with a lavender and black eye. Well-shaped florets. This very pretty cultivar was raised many years ago and is still worthy of a place in the garden.

Summer Wine (M, A, Ex)   Mid-dusky-pink with a white eye. A very reliable plant.

Sungleam (M, A, Ex)   Perhaps the deepest of all the so-called 'yellows'. Certainly the overall appearance is such because of the intense dark true yellow eye. Constitution better than most in this colour range.

Thundercloud (M, A)   Deep purple, black eye. Not the prettiest of delphiniums, but a very vigorous plant capable of producing an abundance of spikes.

Tiddles (M, A)   Lovely slate mauve. No eye, hence a double effect. A most attractive plant for the garden and for floral art.

Wheatear (M, A)   Lavender/purple, darker in the centre. No eye, but almost a double. Very vigorous.

Note   There are other strains offered in seedsmen's catalogues, but you will always be much better off obtaining your seed from strictly reliable sources, such as those mentioned in Appendix III. This list is by no means complete, for new cultivars are added each year to the trial by the Royal Horticultural Society at Wisley, and different and desirable cultivars are always receiving awards. A visit to the trial grounds during June and July is therefore strongly recommended.

Appendices

I LARKSPUR

The larkspur has become the Cinderella of the delphinium world. This is a pity, for when properly grown it can produce a wonderful show in the garden and for floral art it is in much demand.

Seedsmen have found it convenient to list larkspurs currently available under the heading of 'annuals'. This is an incorrect description, for the larkspur is a perennial. It has gained this label, no doubt, because it rarely survives in Britain for more than two years when sown in the autumn and grown as a biennial, and is even more short-lived (living for only one year), when sown in the spring.

There are two recorded species. *D. ajacis* is often referred to as the 'rocket larkspur' and the native plant *D. consolida* is the branching kind. There can be little doubt that the seed generally available today is the result of the hybridisation between the two species. Most of the best strains of seed offered for sale in Britain originated in California where, as with the Pacific strain of delphinium seed, the climate is favourable for hybridisation and the production of seed.

CULTIVATION

Choice of Seed

Although there has not been any substantial trial of larkspur in Britain, there does not appear to be any great advantage in choosing any particular strains offered by the major seedsmen. All can produce a wide range of colours including blue, carmine, rose, lilac, pink and white. They are available in branching form, as well as the taller type which is often referred to as 'Giant Imperial'.

As with delphiniums, it is essential to obtain properly-stored seed. Viability deteriorates quickly when the seed is

132

subjected to high temperatures even for a relatively short period, while freshly-harvested seed will germinate freely and with speed. There are also similarities to the delphinium in the temperature requirements for satisfactory germination. The seed will not normally germinate in temperatures much in excess of 60°F (15°C). By using laboratory techniques of freezing the seed to defined low temperatures for specific periods, it is possible to germinate the seed at higher temperatures, but these skills are beyond the scope of most amateurs.

Sowing

For the finest results, the seed is best sown, where you want the plants to flower, in early October in the north and a couple of weeks later in the south of Britain. A well-drained soil is essential for they will not survive a water-logged environment. Those who garden on a heavy soil should add generous quantities of really sharp sand to the top 2–3in (5–7.5cm) of soil. The young seedlings will survive British winters and can produce magnificent plants the following year, flowering during late May and lasting to the end of June. After flowering the plants will eventually die with the onset of winter, and they are best removed as soon as they begin to look 'tired'.

By contrast, spring-sown seed put into the open soil can more often than not be disappointing, for the plants will never match the magnificence of those that result from autumn-sown seed. Sowing in the spring is not really worth the trouble involved.

There is one other method which can produce fine-quality plants, but a moderately heated glass structure is essential. As the larkspur resents disturbance after germination, to follow the normal practice of pricking out seed from a seed tray into further receptacles is a recipe for failure. Seedlings subjected to this treatment will never recover, and at best will be poor, trivial specimens. The simple secret is to sow a few seeds in a 4in (10cm) pot in January in a temperature of around 50°F (10°C). Providing the seed has been stored at a low temperature, perhaps in a domestic refrigerator, germination will be rapid, and as soon as the seedlings have become large enough to handle they should be thinned to leave just one of the strongest. Grown on in a modest temperature until March, the plants can be planted out after a hardening-off period of a week or two in a frame. These plants will produce spikes every bit as good as the autumn ones sown *in situ*, but will tend to bloom somewhat later, extending the flowering period into July and August.

As with its more glamorous cousins, the *D. elatum*, larkspur has few problems with pests or diseases. Mildew can be a nuisance, but one application of a modern systemic fungicide, as soon as the embryo spike is seen, will give excellent control.

Staking

The taller plants will require some support. To this end, the twiggy type of material used to stake edible peas is ideal and, if it is put in position early on, the foliage of the larkspur will soon hide it from view.

Thinning

When seed is sown in the open ground, which is the case with autumn sowing, then thinning will almost certainly be required. This is best achieved in stages, beginning with a gap of 4in (10cm) between each plant, then increasing this to 8in (20cm) as the plants progress and finally to around 14in (35cm). Using this method is prudent, for it can act as an insurance against the failure of particular plants. If thinning was accomplished to 14in (36cm) in one go, then ugly gaps could occur. It is quite useless to attempt transplanting to fill empty spaces – the plants may well survive, but they will be woefully inferior to those which have not been disturbed.

Conditions

The cultural requirements for larkspur are largely similar to those of *D. elatum*. Do not be fooled into following the advice sometimes advocated that annual flowers do not require rich soil conditions. This may well be true with some annuals which produce vegetative growth at the expense of the flowers, but it is certainly not true for the larkspur. Feed the soil well and the plants will respond.

TREATMENT AFTER FLOWERING

Once flowering is past its best, the sooner the plants are removed the better. They will not flower again and they will not survive to flower the following year. If space is at a premium, a good plan is to fill the vacant site with pot-grown half-hardy plants. One grower of my acquaintance used geraniums (zonal pelargoniums) to very good effect, for it meant he had instant bloom for the rest of the year.

If the intention is to use the same site for a further autumn sowing of larkspur, then of course no further planting can take place. Instead, you will have plenty of time to tidy the area and to add some long-term fertilisers before the October sowing takes place.

The larkspur, so neglected, can be very rewarding. It is probably not popular because so many gardeners try either to transplant the seedlings or to make late spring sowings, both of which will give very poor results indeed. Properly grown they can achieve a spectacular display, and as a cut flower for floral decoration they are superb.

II WHERE TO SEE DELPHINIUMS

In order to keep abreast with the ever-increasing development of the genus, and particularly if one is wishing to start a collection of the latest named cultivars, it is desirable to visit those places where good examples may be viewed. The following observations include fuller details of those places already covered in specific chapters as well as other venues of interest.

WISLEY

The International Trial of Delphiniums

The gardens of the Royal Horticultural Society at Wisley in Surrey must be the first choice for a visit. Those who are members of this august body can visit the garden at almost any time, whereas non-members have restricted visiting

135

hours (details of which should be obtained from the Society beforehand, as there has been a tendency recently for the rules to change). In the trials area many flowers are in the process of being assessed as to their value as garden plants, and high on the list is the large trial of delphiniums.

On average there are about 200 different delphiniums on view and each one is planted in a group of three in order to facilitate judging. Details of the name of each delphinium, the raiser and the introducer may be obtained so that enquiries can be made as to availability for the gardener. Some of the plants will be of very recent introduction, and may be listed under a code description favoured for identification purposes by the raiser. These will almost certainly not be available until the seedling has been successfully judged and a name subsequently registered with the Royal Horticultural Society. In these cases you will need to make a further visit a year later to follow the progress of any particular seedling which has taken your fancy.

A few words of warning are, I feel, necessary for those who have never visited this trial before. The plants are grown exceptionally well; some raisers will go as far as to say that they are grown too well, and that the enormous plants are not really representative. The visitor needs to understand the manner in which they are cultivated in order to appreciate why the average gardener will grow the plants in question in a more modest manner. To begin with, the Royal Horticultural Society chooses a fresh site each year so that there is no danger of a build-up of harmful organisms. If the same site was used year after year, it might lead to an unfair assessment if a particular entry happened to be planted in soil containing, for example, a disease or a pest – this could affect the plant's performance but not that of others in the same trial. Clearly, the Royal Horticultural Society cannot be too careful with such a responsibility. The new site is thoroughly cultivated and liberal quantities of animal manures are incorporated in the soil – probably far more than the average gardener is ever likely to use.

Three rooted cuttings are planted in the spring, and a system of irrigation is installed so that each plant can receive a drip feed of water (which can also contain a solution of plant foods) automatically at specified intervals. It is vital that each and every plant should receive identical attention so that a fair assessment can be made. With this generous treatment the young cuttings make enormous plants in the same year, and these cannot compare with the typical growth experienced by the ordinary gardener or even the enthusiast. In the year which follows this planting the delphiniums are judged and are subjected to an extremely high supplementary diet of plant foods. This rich fare leads to plants capable of producing as many as thirty spikes in just one year, all of them enormous.

The staking of such large plants is a problem on the windswept site and the necessary supports leave a lot to be desired from an aesthetic point of view. The viewer must bear this point in mind when making a personal assessment. In normal garden conditions the plants in question would not have such a rich diet nor would they have been cosseted to such an extent by an automatic drip feed – with normal cultivation the overall height of the plants in the average gardener's plot are bound to be consideraby shorter (although the actual length of the flower spike may well be the same), and will therefore not need so extensive staking. After flowering the plants are then either scrapped or used as stock plants to provide cuttings for the new site. This is a fail-safe system, for special stock plants of each entry are grown elsewhere under normal conditions to provide propagation material. It has been found that, due to the intense cultivation, the plants from the trial ground are invariably unsuitable for this purpose.

Once they know about the unusual cultivation given to these trial plants, visitors are less likely to be overwhelmed by a sight which is truly breathtaking and which always astounds those who view the trial for the first time. One final tip worth mentioning concerns the actual period when the flowers can be seen at their peak of perfection. As with all plants, delphiniums are subject to the vagaries of weather conditions, and the time of blooming will vary from season to season, – it is worthwhile making a telephone enquiry to ascertain when peak blooming is expected.

The University Hybrids

The unique breeding programme of Dr Legro is now also being carried out at Wisley, but the glasshouse where the 'university hybrids' are housed is not open generally, either to Society members or to the public. It is not a display in the normal sense but still part of a scientific breeding programme. There is one occasion when it *may* be possible for the public to view these amazing delphiniums of red, yellow, orange and other similar warm colours, and that is as part of the Delphinium Society's weekend at Wisley.

The Delphinium Society's Weekend at Wisley

For some years this international Society has staged a show at Wisley, which includes a major competition involving its members, as well as other interesting activities. Members will participate, and if there are vacancies non-members are invited to some of the activities.

All visitors to Wisley on that weekend, whether members of the Delphinium Society or not, are made welcome to the display of hundreds of cut spikes entered into the competition. Here you can see all the very best in modern cultivars as well as the latest seedlings raised by leading hybridists, many of which will be on show for the first time. There is an enquiry desk where advice on just about any aspect of the delphinium can be obtained from experts. You will find that the officials of the Society 'on duty' are a very friendly bunch of characters who will be only too willing to share with you all their experiences with the genus. You may well be able to speak to the raiser of many of the delphiniums on view, not only those in the competition but also many of those on the trial ground. There is at least one specialist nurseryman with a trade stand in the competition building, where it is usually possible to purchase seed, as well as young plants in pots, of named cultivars, ready for immediate planting.

There are other events that should not be missed if you have developed a liking for the delphinium. In the past there have been floral arrangement demonstrations and each year there is a conducted tour of the trials. Perhaps the highlight of the weekend is the opportunity to see the 'university hybrids', often with the raiser, Dr Legro, in attendance. This event in particular is always oversubscribed and it pays to book early.

THE LONDON SHOWS

The Delphinium Society usually has a competition at one of the fortnightly shows of the Royal Horticultural Society at Vincent Square, Westminster, London. As the dates vary each year it is essential to make enquiries at the London office, but the shows will usually take place around the 20th June to the 12th July. As at Wisley, the Delphinium Society has an enquiry stand and there is usually at least one specialist nurseryman present with a display of delphiniums and plants to sell.

OUTINGS OF THE DELPHINIUM SOCIETY

One of the privileges of membership of this thriving society is the chance to visit notable gardens or nurseries where delphiniums are a speciality. These events are always popular, for there is no better way than to see delphiniums in actual growth, particularly when they are in association with other flowers and part of the design of a garden.

GARDENS OPEN

A number of amateur gardeners who also specialise in delphiniums open their gardens to members of the Delphinium Society, usually by appointment only. Details are in the *Year Book*, published by the Society, which is free to all members.

Other Societies

In Appendix IV there is a list of local societies which are affiliated to the Delphinium Society. An enquiry to the Secretary will often reveal a delphinium enthusiast living locally who is willing to let you visit his garden, particularly if this enquiry leads to membership.

SPECIALIST NURSERIES

Those nurseries mentioned on page 140 are well worth a visit towards the end of June. You will be able to see large collections of named cultivars as well as some seedlings raised for trial purposes. It is usually possible to purchase plants at the same time which will be at a stage ready for planting out into a permanent site.

Visitors are usually welcome. However, because most of

these are family businesses, it is prudent to telephone first to ensure that someone is available to see you.

CHELSEA FLOWER SHOW

Blackmore & Langdon never fail to produce a wonderful display for Chelsea Flower Show of delphiniums, all grown in containers. Orders for plants are accepted on their stand, for delivery through the mail, or for collection at their nursery.

A visit to the Delphinium Society's stand is always worthwhile. Many publications are available, as well as seed for sale, demonstrations of seed sowing and vegetative propagation. Any question on the genus will result in expert advice from members of the enthusiastic committee in attendance.

III SUPPLIERS OF PLANTS AND SEEDS

The Delphinium Society (seed available to members)

Blackmore & Langdon
Pensford
Near Bristol

Harrisons Delphiniums
Newbury Cottage
Playhatch
Reading RG4 9QN

Rougham Hall Nurseries
Ipswich Road
Rougham
Bury St Edmunds
(September/October delivery.)

Woodfield Brothers
71 Townsend Road
Tiddington
Stratford-on-Avon
(No despatch facilities)

The following are enthusiasts who have some plants and seed for sale:

Dr David Bassett
'Takakkaw'
Ice House Wood, Oxted,
Surrey RH8 9DW
(Hand-pollinated seed to colour. Seed sent by post world-wide. A limited quantity of rooted cuttings of their own introductions as well as selected named cultivars. Mail-order sales accepted, but for United Kingdom only. No callers without appointment.)

Roy Latty
Ashton
Deanland, Sixpenny Handley,
Dorset SP5 5PD

Duncan McGlashan
47 Victoria Hill Road, Hextable, Swanley,
Kent
(Wide range of hand-pollinated seed available, also a range of rooted cuttings. Seed sent world-wide. No callers without appointment.)

Nigel Moody
98 Station Road, Bretforton, Near Evesham,
Worcestershire
(An experimental garden with hundreds of hand-crossed seedlings on view. No callers without appointment.)

Stuart Ogg
Hopton, Fletching Street, Mayfield,
East Sussex TN20 6TL

IV NATIONAL AND INTERNATIONAL SOCIETIES

THE DELPHINIUM SOCIETY

The Secretary
R Joslyn
5 Woodfield Avenue, Carshalton Beeches,
Surrey SM5 3JB

Membership Secretary
Mrs S. A. Bassett
'Takakkaw'
Ice House Wood
Oxted
Surrey RH8 9DW

THE DELPHINIUM SOCIETY

One of the aims of this international society, founded over sixty years ago, is to encourage members, especially amateurs, to raise new cultivars. To this end much information is available in its publications and in its annual 120-page year book. The society is affiliated to the Royal Horticultural Society and there is much friendly co-operation in the further-ance of the development of this genus.

Over the sixty years there have been many changes. When first formed in 1928 it was really a society for the horticultural trade. The dominant members were around 44 professional growers who specialised almost exclusively in the genus, and it was they who influenced most of the decision-making and stood to gain from a thriving society.

This domination continued up to the outbreak of the Second World War, but from 1945 changes began to take place astonishingly quickly. The number of specialist del-phinium nurseries dwindled and after a few years just one remained – Messrs Blackmore & Langdon. The admin-istration of the Delphinium Society was now conducted by amateurs, and this time also marked the beginning of the amateur's attempt to raise new delphiniums. This trend has continued, and now most new cultivars come from the gardener – none in recent years have come from commerce.

SOCIETIES AFFILIATED TO THE DELPHINIUM SOCIETY

Great Britain

The voluntary officials who administer each society often change every twelve months, so it could be misleading to give a contact address. However, each society is well known at local level, and a current address can, more often than not, be obtained from a local public library. The Membership Secretary of the Delphinium Society will always be pleased to give particulars on receipt of a stamped addressed envelope.

Ainsdale Horticultural Society, Southport, Merseyside
Alderley Edge and Wilmslow Horticultural and Rose Society, Wilmslow, Cheshire
Alresford and District Horticultural Society, Alresford, Hampshire
Banstead Horticultural Society, Banstead, Surrey
Barnet Horticultural Society, Barnet, Hertfordshire
British Airways Clubs Horticultural Society, Heathrow Airport
Bromley and District Horticultural Society, Bromley, Kent
Bushey, Bushey Heath and District Horticultural Society, Watford, Hertfordshire
Chandlers Ford and District Gardeners Club, Eastleigh, Hampshire
Chingford Horticultural Society, Chingford, Essex
Chiswick Horticultural Society, Chiswick, London
Cuffley Horticultural Society, Potters Bar, Hertfordshire
Coutts Horticultural Society, London
Finchley Horticultural Society, Woodside Park, London
Hatchend Horticultural Society, Pinner, Middlesex
Haywards Heath Horticultural Society, Haywards Heath, Sussex
Headley Horticultural Society, Bordon, Hampshire
Hitchin Horticultural Society, Letchworth, Hampshire
Hutton Horticultural Society, Brentwood, Essex
Ickenham and Swakeleys Horticultural Society, Uxbridge, Middlesex
Langton Green and District Horticultural Society, Tunbridge Wells, Kent
Kingswood, Walton and Tadworth Horticultural Society, Tadworth, Surrey

Marlow and District Horticultural Society, Marlow, Buckinghamshire
Merrow Horticultural Society, Guildford, Surrey
Middlesex Show Society, Uxbridge, Middlesex
Naphill Horticultural Society, High Wycombe, Buckinghamshire
North Tonbridge Horticultural Society, Tonbridge, Kent
Norwich and Norfolk Horticultural Society, Norwich, Norfolk
Northern Horticultural Society, Harrogate, Yorkshire
Pinner Horticultural Society, Pinner, Middlesex
Sanderstead Horticultural Society, Sanderstead, Surrey
Saxlingham and District Horticultural Society, Norwich, Norfolk
Shalford, Chilworth and Peasmarsh Gardening Club, Guildford, Surrey
Southgate and District Horticultural Society, Winchmore Hill, London
Southport Recreation and Amenities Department, Borough of Southport, Lancashire
Surbiton Horticultural Society, Chessington, Surrey
Surrey Horticultural Federation, Surrey
Sutton and District Horticultural Society, Sutton, Surrey
Thames Valley Horticultural Society, Staines, Middlesex
Wallington, Carshalton and Beddington Horticultural Society, Wallington, Surrey
Weybridge Horticultural Club, Godalming, Surrey
Worcester Park Horticultural Society, Worcester Park, Surrey

Overseas

Canterbury Horticultural Society, New Zealand
Hutt Valley Horticultural Society, New Zealand
Transvaal Horticultural Society, South Africa
Western Reserve Delphinium Society, Cleveland, Ohio, USA

The membership of the Delphinium Society is world-wide, and it currently has members who reside in the following countries:

Argentina, Australia, Belgium, Canada, Eire, France, Germany, Holland, India, Israel, Italy, Japan, Kenya,

Luxembourg, Mauritius, New Zealand, Norway, South
Africa, Spain, Swaziland, Sweden, Switzerland, United
States of America, Zimbabwe.

V GLOSSARY

Anthers   A part of the male portion of a flower which bears
the pollen, situated at the top of the stamen.
Back cross   Crossing a hybrid back with one of its parents.
Bee   A term often used to describe the eye of a delphinium,
because of its similarity, on some species, to the insect of the
same name.
Belladonnas   A race distinct from *D. elatum*, partly derived
from *D. belladonna*.
Breeding   A deliberate attempt in hybridisation to create a
new break when using two different cultivars.
Capillary action   The force which enables liquids (in horticultural parlance) to be drawn up through soil particles.
Compost   The ingredients which, when mixed together,
form the growing media for sowing seed or for potting
plants. The term is also used for vegetable waste matter
which is placed in a heap to rot down to supply valuable
humus for enriching the soil.
Chromosomes   Part of the nucleus which carry the genes of a
cell. The number of chromosomes can vary enormously
from genus to genus and also within a genus, making cross-
pollination almost unlikely.
Crown   The hard portion of root structure of a delphinium
from which new shoots form.
Cultivar   The term introduced by the Royal Horticultural
Society in June 1964 to replace the word 'variety'.
Cutting   The young shoot removed from the crown when it
is 2–3in (5–7.5cm) high, devoid of roots, but which may be
induced to form roots when placed in a suitable environment
(such as a compost).
Dominant   Term used to describe a feature which constantly
reappears whenever the same cultivar is used as one of the
parents of a cross.
Elatum   The term used to describe all garden delphiniums
commonly grown.
Embryo   The undeveloped spike of a delphinium, either
when it is first discernible, or when it is in the process of
being formed.

Eye The innermost part of a floret. It is the whole of the anthers when fully open, and is also known as the 'bee'.

F1 hybrid If a cross is made between the same two parents and the progeny are similar each time the cross is carried out, the resultant seedlings are said to be F1 hybrids.

Floret The whole of a single bloom on a delphinium spike.

Formaldehyde A total chemical steriliser, which kills nearly all plant life and soil organisms.

Fungicide A chemical designed to combat many plant diseases, notably mildew in delphiniums.

Hermaphrodite In horticultural terms, a creature with characteristics of both male and female (for example, a slug).

Hormone powder A compound designed to assist the formation of roots on a rootless cutting.

Hybrid The progeny of a cross made between two different cultivars.

Fasciation A physiological disorder, when cells of a plant become irregular in the mass, leading to distorted growth, often in grotesque forms.

John Innes composts Tried and tested, reliable formulae for the blending of materials to form plant composts.

Line breeding The selection of the best progeny of a cross to be used in a further cross and, the best progeny of that cross, yet again used in a further cross. This is repeated for as long as may be required and establishes a line in breeding.

Maiden A plant blooming for the first time, usually one year old.

Metaldehyde A highly poisonous chemical used in preparations to destroy slugs.

Methiocarb A chemical, said to be less dangerous (although no proof exists) than metaldehyde, for destroying slugs and their eggs. It is also generally agreed among horticulturalists to be far more effective.

Micro-propagation A laboratory method of plant propagation, where minute portions of plant tissue are placed in a culture and are induced to form extremely tiny plants.

Mist propagation A method of rooting cuttings. They are placed under glass where, at regular intervals, a fine mist spray of water is directed around them by automatic equipment, thereby replacing the lost moisture content of the cutting. Not successful with delphiniums.

Molluscs Soft-bodied animals, including those with hard outer shells. The common examples in horticulture are slugs and snails.

Open-pollinated When a plant bears seed which has been formed without interference by man, such seed is open-pollinated. When this natural process is interfered with by man, as in hybridisation, the seed obtained is no longer open-pollinated.

Organic Tricky to define as its horticultural meaning is not strictly accurate. By and large the term refers to materials found in nature as opposed to man-made substances. Peat, garden compost and animal residues are considered to be organic, whereas sulphate of ammonia, sulphate of iron and sulphate of potash are said to be inorganic.

Perennial A plant which is normally capable of living for more than two years. The elatum delphinium is a perennial.

Perlite A product used in place of sand in composts to keep it 'open'. Absorbs water rather like a sponge and is also very useful for rooting cuttings.

Pollination The action of transferring pollen from the anthers to the stigma, either naturally or by artificial means, in order to achieve fertilisation

Progeny The relationship with descendants. In horticultural terms, the plants obtained from the result of fertilisation – a plant's offspring.

Protandrous The ability (of slugs) to change their sex and become hermaphrodite.

Recessive Describes the failure of a particular feature in a selected parent to reappear each time a cross is made with another cultivar.

Self-fertile The ability of a plant to set seed from its own pollen.

Sepal One of the petals which form the whole floret.

Shoot The new growth which comes from the crown of the plant, which is below the surface of the soil.

Side-Shoot A term sometimes used incorrectly to denote a lateral.

Species A wild plant.

Spike The whole of the flowering portion made up of individual florets.

Stigma The receptive part of a floret. When it becomes sticky any pollen which adheres to the surface will achieve fertilisation.

Stool The mass of the root system including the crown.

Systemic A plant liquid, usually an insecticide, which is so manufactured that the poisonous ingredients are absorbed through the plant tissues. Thus when an insect feeds on the leaves it will consume some of the insecticide and die. The effect may remain viable for as long as several weeks.

Variety Because it was never defined, the term 'variety' caused so much confusion among horticulturalists that 'cultivar' was substituted in 1968. However, many uninformed gardeners and, indeed, nurserymen still use the original term.

Vermiculite A useful material for rooting cuttings and for adding to composts in place of peat and sand. It has the ability to hold a large amount of moisture, but at the same time adequate supplies of air are maintained.

Viability Seed which has retained its powers of germination is said to have maintained its viability.

Virus A plant disease. Can attack delphiniums and can be recognised by a narrowing of the foliage – in extreme cases the florets also exhibit this characteristic.

Note The author is well aware that some of the definitions given are narrow in concept. The emphasis has been to confine descriptions as applicable to the delphinium.

VI FURTHER READING

The Delphinium, Frank Bishop (Collins, 1949)
Delphiniums, Colin Edwards (Dent, 1981)
Delphiniums, Roy Genders (John Gifford, 1963)
The Book of the Delphinium, John Leeming (Pitman, 1932)
Delphiniums for Everyone, Stuart Ogg (Blandford, 1961)
Delphiniums, Ronald Parrett (Penguin, 1961)
Delphiniums, George Phillips (Eyre & Spottiswoode, 1949)
Delphiniums and Campanulas, A G Puttock (John Gifford, 1973)

General Index

General Index

Methiocarb 66
Michaelmas Daisy 117
Micro-propagation 52
Mildew 69, 111
Mini trial of seed 37
Mist propagation 52
Moving house 113
Mulching 58

Naming 74, 77
Nitrogen 97

One colour border 117, 118
Open pollination 23, 26

pH values 55
Pacific Giants 16
Parrett, Ronald 18
Peat 56
Perlite 36, 51
Pinching out 101, 106
Planting 37
  schemes 115
Potash 102, 104
Preparation for show purposes 85
Preservatives for cut spikes 85

Recessive qualities 25
Red delphiniums 20, 21
Refrigeration of seed 36
Registration of seedlings 74
Reinelt, Frank 15
Root system 37
Rooted cuttings 195
Rooting cuttings 49
Roses 117
Rot 69
Royal Horticultural Society 41, 74, 75, 108, 135
Sand 51
Scrabbling 48, 98
Second blooming 60, 111
Seed 30, 114

Seedlings 36, 105, 109
Selection for exhibition 81
  of seedlings 40
Self-fertile 23, 26
Short plants 58
Showing 81
Siting of plants 56
Slugs 64, 96, 97, 101
  bait 65, 66
Snails 64
Soil, preparation 55
  sickness 68
Specialist nurserymen 140, 141
Species 122–126
Spring sowing 34, 99
Staging at shows 87
Staking 57, 80, 102
Stock plants 114
Stopping 101
Storage of seed 29, 30

Temperature 32, 34, 51
Thinning 57, 79, 97
Timing for exhibition 81
Tortrix moth 67
Transplanting 31
Travelling 86
Trials of delphiniums 74

University Hybrids 20, 21, 137
United States of America 15

Vegetative propagation 47
Vegetable plot 120
Vermiculite 36
Veronica 'Shirley Blue' 118
Viability of seed 36
Virus 70

Water cuttings 50
Watering 38, 58, 80, 103
Windy sites 58

Index of Species and Cultivars